Searching for Love

Girls and grown women made Elvis a star. They felt the impact of his good looks and suave personality. They recognized that behind the leer, extravagant costumes, the insinuating voice of a performer who entertained with his whole body, a kid so sexy he had to be shown on TV from the waist up, there lay a sensitive, simple youth searching for the same experiences as they were—love and honest affection.

Other books by David Hanna:

ELVIS

LONELY STAR AT THE TOP

David Hanna

LEISURE BOOKS   •   NEW YORK CITY

A LEISURE BOOK

Published by

Nordon Publications, Inc.
Two Park Avenue
New York, N.Y. 10016

for
Aimée Torriani Ryder

Chapter 1

"He was the only king we ever had," sighed the fortyish, balding man as he slipped on his light summer jacket over his short sleeved shirt, snapped off the radio in the skyscraper office where he worked as a commercial artist. It was a job he'd held for almost as many years as Elvis Presley had been a superstar in the American entertainment scene, outclassing, outperforming, outgrossing all pretenders to his throne with the ease of a giant swatting a fly off his shoulder.

He'd had his problems in the two decades plus he'd been before the public; marital, the usual paternity suit male celebrities face, a few years away for a tour with the U.S. Army and in recent years, illness. But somehow the King had always come back.

The advertising man said, "I don't want to hear any more. It's like losing a friend you once loved and never forget even if you see him less frequently as the years roll by. It happens all the time. You begin to expect it. But Elvis? Forty-two! That's cutting it pretty fine."

At the city desk of a suburban newspaper, the grey-haired, middle-aged newspaperman on duty glanced at the copy turned in by the paper's "bright, young hope"—one of many kids finding good jobs on newspapers around the country today as publishers struggle to keep their publications alive by bringing America's old, tired journals into the last quarter of the Twentieth Century. He'd been assigned the "commentary" on Presley's passing. The editor glanced at the copy, reading the first line, "Elvis Presley died suddenly yesterday afternoon and a whole generation was plunged into..."

The editor knew it was a hackneyed lead and if he'd told his young reporters once, he'd told them a thousand times that death is always *sudden*, it happens in a fraction of a second—that people die *unexpectedly*. "But what the hell," he muttered, "let it go. What else is there to say. Elvis? I guess you'd call it *sudden death*."

Elvis Presley was the King—the King of Rock 'n' Roll. He was a superstar who had been at the top of the charts for twenty-two years, earning millions of dollars for himself, more millions for his promoters. At the same time he enchanted millions of people. They were the young people of the fifties who loved him on sight; their elders, who loathed him. But time and Elvis worked their magic. As Elvis raced through an almost incredible catalogue of work, hundreds of records and albums, more than two dozen movies, scores of television, night club and stadium appearances, the old animosities had disappeared.

It was hard to imagine on that humid Wednesday afternoon that Elvis had ever provoked controversy, so genuinely moved were Americans everywhere, of every age and disposition, at his untimely death.

"It doesn't make sense. It's not right. What happened?" they kept saying to one another, with the very real feeling that they had a very personal stake in Elvis' life and fortunes.

True, there were the rumors, his collapse after a fairly recent performance, secret trips to Memphis and the hospital, and a tawdry book intended to destroy Elvis' image of *Mr. Clean*. The last was dismissed by Elvis fans, now mature and reasonable adults, who chose to remember how, in the 1950's, they had handed Elvis his *Laurel Wreath*, crowning him the King—a wreath he'd worn with style, modesty, charisma and giant-sized talent during his years before the public.

According to ancient protocol a King may neither be born or die alone—but in the presence of his Royal Court. Although Elvis' birth took place before a handful of his mother's good friends, neighbors all anxious to help the pretty young woman through her first experience at giving birth, Elvis, in a sense was born alone.

There was no question that he died alone. The King was found unconscious in the bathroom of the splendid pink and white palace he had built for himself and his family in Memphis, Tennessee, called Graceland, at two-thirty in the afternoon, August 16, 1977, by his road manager, Joe Esposito.

Esposito called the Memphis Fire Department

and after resuscitation efforts failed, the attendants eased him onto a stretcher, carried him to an ambulance and raced to the Baptist Memorial Hospital, only ten minutes away.

Elvis was dead before he left Graceland and in the hour the hospital's elite cardiac arrest team worked over him, his body was already turning blue. An hour later the King was pronounced dead. At four-thirty, the news was released to the press, spinning its way around the world in big, black headlines. The greatest, most touched mourners abroad were those in England who kept asking, "Why didn't Elvis ever perform here? How we would have loved him!"

An entire nation, headed by President Jimmy Carter who sent a telegram of condolence to the Presley family, mourned an idol who had enjoyed their adulation for so long that Elvis was part of their lives, an entertainer who had come out of nowhere to be hailed as an original, an innovator, a style-setter on the one hand; a crude, vulgar, noisy exhibitionist on the other.

Elvis brought originality and vitality to the vapid, lifeless music of the fifties. His was not the slick, familiar performance of a performer in tux, straw hat and cane doing standards, punctuating the lyrics with flashes of capped white teeth. Elvis was a gutsy young man looking for something fresh and new, in style, music, arrangements and presentation.

Elvis projected sensuous vibes that began weaving magic in the appearance of the singer himself. His soft face seemed to hide a cynicism, an inner hardness, balanced by his deep, gentle blue eyes. The slick, black pompadour was wild and far-out. Elvis' movements were feline, graceful, sensuously provocative as they climaxed in bumps and grinds that old-timers claimed reduced the gyrations of famed stripper Carrie Finnell to a pirouette on the White House lawn.

Elvis, with his long side-burns, skin-tight pink and white costumes, lips curled in a sneer, oozed a new kind of sex appeal. It was right on the line. No kidding around—and young girls were the first to know what he was telling them. They squealed, they groaned, they fainted. They cried, bit their handkerchiefs into pieces and it wasn't long before *Elvis the Pelvis* had wrapped up the younger male generation as well.

But the suggestive nickname, the style, the clothes, the manner, the impudence, the sneer and the curl of Elvis' lip were all anathema to parents and church groups who considered the sudden rage for Elvis Presley as "disgraceful." Not since the heydays of Mae West's battles with censors in the movies and radio had there been such a hoopla about a performer. Back in the fifties when Elvis' name was synonomous with the devil's, no one could imagine a president of the United States saying, "We have lost a friend. My whole family and I thought of him as a friend."

There have been a great many changes in the world since Elvis was born on January 8, 1935 in Tupelo, Mississippi, when the President was not a peanut farmer from Georgia but a gentleman farmer, Franklin D. Roosevelt, who was born in the manner of royalty and aristocracy in the family's home at Hyde Park, New York, where the whole Roosevelt clan was assembled to welcome its newest member.

In Washington, Roosevelt was wrestling with the problems of an aggravating, persistent Depression that would not go away and reached into virtually every American home. The Great Depression was not as discriminating as the usual economic recession. It touched rich and poor alike but, needless to say, for every Wall Street broker who threw himself out of the window of a New York skyscraper, there were millions of impoverished Americans who would have been satisfied just having windows.

The Great Depression was harshest in the big cities and in the rural areas of the south. Both were dependent on seasonal occupations and small businesses for survival.

In the north, unions were attempting to organize industries whose owners harbored such deep fears of organized labor that they readily succumbed to the blandishments of gangsters who alternately sold them protection and, representing the workers on the other side, manufactured "sweetheart" contracts that satisfied no one and only enriched the hoods.

Dairy farmers were pouring milk onto the highways and in the mid-west and south, farmers burned their crops rather than sell them at the low price offered in the market place.

For people of Tupelo, life meant a constant battle for survival—against the elements and an economy that held out little hope. What, they wondered, would it provide for their children? They worried, they doubted, they feared. But with the eternal optimism of humanity, they carried on the activities of life, working, worshipping, marrying, sometimes feuding, but always helping one another in times of deep distress.

It was not a pretty world that greeted Elvis in the clapboard shanty of East Tupelo, Mississippi, where the houses were built on stilts to protect them from seasonal floods. His father, Vernon Presley, was twenty-one when he married Gladys Smith. He built their shanty with his own hands. It was a shade better than most found in the neighborhood because it featured a porch rather than a stoop. Vernon had worked hard and long in the fields to buy materials to build the house. After their marriage, Gladys worked as a sewing machine operator to supplement their income.

Tupelo, Mississippi lies in one of those areas of the south threatened either by the sun or by floods. The land is spare and rocky. The crops are cotton and sugarcane—hard fields to work in the best of times; almost beyond human endurance in the era of the Depression.

A year after Elvis' birth, a tornado whirled through Tupelo, destroying numerous homes and killing more than a hundred people. But the wooden shack built by Vernon Presley survived—with its sturdy plank floor, outhouse, a few windows, an outdoor pump and the porch in which the family took such pride.

Vernon Presley possessed skills far beyond those of a sharecropper or field hand—jobs that necessity obliged him to take. He was a fine carpenter and house painter. But the men of Tupelo did their own carpentry and were too poor to afford paint—much less a painter.

More than anything else, Vernon wanted Gladys' first born to begin life in a hospital. He worked harder than ever to collect enough money, especially after they knew that Gladys was bearing twins.

There were varying accounts of the reasons Gladys didn't make it to a hospital—the tradition that all Presleys were born at home, or that the local doctor pooh-poohed the idea. Vernon Presley was a decisive man. If he could have afforded a hospital, he would have gotten his wife there. Sufficient money simply did not exist.

So Elvis, like all Tupelo babies, was born at home with neighborhood women assisting. Elvis was the first to arrive in a difficult birth and for several hours after, his life hung in the balance. The second child, also a boy, was born dead.

There is an old belief about a "mirror baby"—that the surviving member of a dual birth is possessed of unusual psychic strength but is only half a person because he needs his twin for total strength. Thus, Elvis was born, as he died, *alone*—without the brother who belonged to him.

*　　　*　　　*

He was given the middle name "Aron" which had been reserved for his brother. Gladys Presley mourned the death of Aron as much as she rejoiced in the birth of Elvis. She knew she had borne her one and only child so Elvis became the couple's very special baby. Gladys even gave up her job to spend more time with her son—a decision not taken lightly by a young couple whose combined income amounted to approximately thirty dollars a week.

But folks "made out" during the Depression. The terrible economic disaster brought people together as never before—or since. The life of the poor people in Tupelo revolved around the church and its activities. There was no money for anything else—not even movies which were cheap.

The Presleys didn't drink, so that pleasure was automatically eliminated, saving both money and lots of heartache. Young people with children simply created their own amusements. Besides the church, there was the radio, a blessing that might have been invented especially for the Depression.

It offered the greatest entertainers in the world, music of every variety, the classics in the dramatic repertory, and an endless list of daily soap operas. "Graduates" of the Depression recall the radio with the affection reserved for an old and good friend—one that never disappointed. It was always there, sometimes good, sometimes superb; frequently awful, but it didn't run off and leave you in the lurch.

Nor did the church. Gladys Presley and her husband were not excessively religious but they were members of the *Fundamentalist Assembly of the Church of God* which they attended frequently, if not regularly.

The Presleys could always be counted on to

participate in church affairs. In church, Elvis and Gladys began discovering each other—and Elvis first noticed the world beyond his mother's arms. He began singing—or humming—at an early age. Gladys encouraged him.

Gladys' devotion to Elvis marked his entire life. When he was young, schoolmates teased him and called him a "mamma's boy." When she died, there were those who said that Elvis was never the same afterward. He never stopped missing her or expressing his affection for her.

In the social environment of a small town, there was importance in the companionship of a mother and her baby. Besides household chores and attending to the needs of her husband, that composed her life. The family! It was the beginning and the end of their existence so every detail of Elvis' babyhood stood out in Gladys' mind.

Later, she told people how Elvis would run out of his seat during services, trying to reach the choir and sing with them. She maintained that he could carry a tune at three.

Pleasing his mother seemed important to Elvis and one finds him an affable child—willing to go with her and do anything she said. There was, for example, none of a child's natural reluctance to go to church in Elvis. He frankly enjoyed it. But to assume that he was excessively spiritual or intended for the ministry is nowhere substantiated. Elvis found more than average pleasure in churchgoing—largely because of the singing.

Vernon Presley, like many farmers, was a good

whistler. It was a way of keeping going during the long hours of work. So when Elvis was not in school he used to follow his father into the fields and whistle along with him.

Then, there was the radio. Elvis, like all kids of the time, spent hours listening to the array of programs that poured forth—the best entertainment available in the world.

The world of radio was filled with music, and Elvis hummed the songs along with the name entertainers of the day and at night, even as kids in the city, Elvis was able to dream his dreams.

Quite early he made up his mind to be a singer, an entertainer of some sort. Neither his mother or father discouraged him. The Depression was not the era to discourage dreams—however outrageous they might seem to an obscure sharecropper's family hidden away in a clapboard house on stilts in the south.

Dreams were free and to dream was to escape the cold realities of the time. Young Depression parents were tough and resilient. They had to be. They didn't ask where "their children were." They knew. Kids were their reason for living, the key to their survival. If Gladys and Vernon Presley today appear overprotective of their child, they were typical of millions in the same position. Parents readily denied themselves in order that "the kids wouldn't know the suffering we're going through."

Daily, Gladys walked Elvis to school from the time he was five years old. Both parents drilled manners into him that persisted to the day he died.

Women were addressed as "Ma'am" and men were called "Sir." He was careful always to say "please" and "thank you."

He never interrupted a conversation and met new people with cool politeness and respect. Basically, Elvis was shy and it must have taken enormous effort on his part—and his parents'—to draw him out of his shell. Obviously the Presleys were far from ordinary people. They appear to have possessed a perception of their child's gifts and allowed him to explore them freely. In this respect Elvis was lucky.

*   *   *

The first ten years of Elvis' life were marked by grinding poverty. Jobs became scarcer and both Vernon and Gladys aged in appearance far beyond their years while Elvis, early photos reveal, was anything but handsome, a chubby little boy.

Elvis was a homely child. His large broad nose seemed out of proportion and his fleshy lips seemed to be distorted in an off-center sneer. As he matured, however, these features lost their awkwardness. By the time he was in high school, he had become a handsome young man.

His world was small, but Elvis learned how to make the best of it. He wandered across the land, exercised his imagination, made up games to play by himself. Always there was the radio and the pleasure he found in singing along with it.

He was a lonely child, but so were millions of

other Depression children. Poor kids, with nothing to share, swap, or experiences to talk about, are reluctant to seek out other poor kids. They've been nowhere so what was there to talk about? As far as they could see, they were going nowhere.

Luckily, a child makes his own life or, like their elders, the Depression kids would have taken to drink or flung themselves out of windows. In the bleak land around Tupelo, there must have been a quicksand pit a kid could have dumped himself into.

Although both the Presley and Smith families had lived in the region for generations, they'd managed to acquire little that would tide the young parents over the difficult early years of Elvis' childhood. They lost their home, moving several times, often in the middle of the night. With each move, their domestic environment deteriorated but the Presleys could say, in happier years, there was always food on the table. That was the hallmark of accomplishment in the Depression. To those who remember the thirties, it was a considerable one.

Elvis was encouraged to sing by his teachers and he became a featured attraction at school events. When he was ten Elvis entered the annual singing contest of the Mississippi-Alabama Fair. Standing on a chair the child sang an old country standard, Red Foley's *Old Shep*, and won a five-dollar second prize.

The win also entitled Elvis to free admission to all the rides at the park, and from that day on, Elvis was devoted to amusement parks. He liked to rent them out for parties and, at the time of his death, was making an arrangement for an amusement park shindig.

The youngster's success at the fair produced his first guitar, bought from a mail order house for $12.50. It was probably the best investment he ever made. There were uncles in the family to help Elvis with the rudiments of the instrument, but it didn't take him long to figure out chords and harmonies and begin playing on his own.

In 1948, Vernon Presley decided that he had given all he could to the society he'd been born into. He was thirty-four with a wife and an adolescent son to support. There was no place else for them to go in Tupelo. He'd lost his own home with the "porch" and now they had become as close to "squatters" as a man of Vernon's dignity could tolerate.

They were living close to the ghetto and saw no way of improving things. Job after job had slipped away from Vernon's hands because business remained stubbornly depressed, and making out as an odd-job man simply didn't meet the bills.

So the rural Presley family, like millions of others, decided they would have to take a big and fateful move—head for a city. The nearest big one was Memphis, Tennessee. They packed up and moved in 1948, just in time for Elvis to enter high school, having completed junior high in his birthplace.

*   *   *

His parents brought to Memphis both disappointments and hopes.

Young Elvis carried more, hopes, dreams, a guitar and by no means accidentally, a preparation for his career that couldn't have been bought at any price— one that the Presleys and Tupelo had made possible; keeping him clothed and fed, teaching him manners, taking him to church where he could sing and learn the words of the spirituals, and letting the youngster have ready access to the magic box, the radio.

Here he could listen to and study the big country singers of the day, Roy Acuff, Ernie Tubbs, Weaver Brothers and Elviry, Judy Canova; the great black men who sand the "blues"—fabled names like Big Bill Broonzy, Otis Span, B.B. King, John Lee Hooker. There were the Broadway names as well— Jolson, Cantor, Harry Richman, Crosby, Vallee, Perry Como and Frank Sinatra. And not to be overlooked was all the whistling he'd done out in the fields with his father.

Had young Elvis studied singing in the city he'd never have run into such an opportunity to develop his lung power—and what's more—without even thinking about it.

Frank Sinatra spent hours early in his career exercising breath control. Richard Burton's uncle took him out into the fields in Wales and made him recite Shakespeare against the wind. John Carradine used to sneak into the Hollywood Bowl at night to declaim the Bard and create the resonant voice that led to his successful film and stage career.

Elvis was doing naturally what professionals paid fortunes to master. All that youthful whistling, psalm singing, humming along with the radio had given Elvis lung power, a sense of phrasing and timing. All so effortlessly achieved but part of the grand scheme that would lead the barefoot boy from Mississippi to the heights as a sensuous cyclone— one of the most enduring and successful Show Business personalities ever known.

His face began to shape into the handsome young man the public would meet in a few short years. His eyes brightened, he began to find that lean, eager, sexy look and already Elvis showed maturity beyond his years. He was no longer all arms and legs, but a young man in total possession of his body, a strong young fellow who'd learn karate later and had begun to achieve control of his movements.

Most of all, he brought with him the gift of self-containment. He had learned to live by himself and within himself. It could also be called loneliness— depending on where you are when it's mentioned.

A child doesn't dwell too much on loneliness while it's happening. It only occurs to him later on— especially when he's famous and asked a thousand and one times to describe his childhood.

"We were broke, man," he'd say. "Dad just packed our things one night, put them on top of our old battered Plymouth and off we went. We headed for Memphis, hoping things would be better."

Elvis was old enough now to realize how rough a life his parents had led. He'd seen them working from dawn until late at night, scratching to pick up what amounted to pennies.

Elvis had no idea how he could help once they got

to Memphis. But he intended to. He'd never been far from home and had no notion of what life looked like in a big city. From the radio he figured it was noisy; from the few movies he'd seen, it was full of people always rushing from one place to another.

You couldn't say that Elvis had promised himself to be a success—or even that he was going to find a job to help his parents. He knew he was big for his age, strong physically, and that he'd be attending high school. He was another Depression kid moving on.

Elvis wasn't aware that he was going to the right place at the right time.

Chapter 2

Memphis was a colorful city. For years it had enjoyed high marks in the critical eyes of theatrical people who judged a town by their acceptance of entertainment and the quality of entertainment to be found in it.

High on the list was the quality of Tennessee's corn *likker* during Prohibition and that Beale Street simply opened the doors of its saloons once the Eighteenth Amendment had been repealed. They'd never really closed. The city's famed jazz pianists in new faces with up-to-date arrangements were still at the stools of the battered uprights making music they called the *Memphis Blues*.

Legitimate theatre companies could always depend on two, maybe three good weeks in Memphis. In the great days of vaudeville it was a valuable and important city to play. If they liked an act there, Memphis was the key to the lush booking time available throughout the south.

Music—jazz and the blues—gave Memphis its special place in the affection of show people. They loved to listen and the white entertainers often wondered why so few of them knew how to use it.

Al Jolson did. So did Blossom Seeley. But they were the exceptions. Somehow when you got away from the black jazz saloons of New Orleans, Memphis, Chicago's South Side, the blues got mixed up with "torch singing"—an expression coined by Broadway columnist Louis Sobel to describe Tommy Lyman, a saloon singer who came close to the style of intimate entertainment found in the black cabarets of the pre-war era.

For Elvis, Memphis emerged a gaudy kaleidoscope of sight, sound and bigness far beyond his comprehension. To him the streets seemed endless, and it was strange to find so many people concentrated in small areas—like the downtown business district where the Presleys found their first shabby apartment. It wasn't easy to get used to and Elvis, more than the average country boy, had been protected. His shyness, always haunting him, became more pronounced.

Until he came to Memphis, Elvis had never seen a bathroom built into a home. The discovery was a marvel. Gladys actually would have preferred the water pump and outside privy. The bathroom, its sink with water taps, had to serve as her kitchen sink, as well as the place where she stored her dishes after cooking the family's meals on an electric stove.

Their first home was once a gracious mansion which had been converted into apartments. There may have been a time when they were perfectly respectable and well maintained. But in these post-war years, when properties had been allowed to deteriorate, the place was in horrible condition. The electrical wiring was woefully inadequate and dangerous. There was no heat to speak of in winter, and the Presley family huddled together in one room like so many cattle. They were three of sixty people crowded into the building.

Life in the Big City looked anything but promising, since Vernon remained in the same position that he'd been in for years, grabbing day work when he could until 1949 when he went to work as a laborer in the United Paint Company, packing cans of paint for shipment. Vernon's wages came to $38.50 a week—on weeks when he was lucky enough to draw overtime.

Sometimes Vernon and Gladys questioned their judgment in moving to the big town but with time, things straightened out. They were interviewed by the Memphis Housing Authority. After the usual red tape, they were accepted in a Federal Housing Authority building where the rent was twenty-five dollars a month.

Still, it was hard going. Vernon's back had begun to fail him; the years in the fields had taken their toll. He realized he could expect no improvement in the labor market. He'd have to stay where he was, in an unskilled low-paying job.

Elvis was enrolled in L.C. Hume High School and, as she had in Tupelo, Gladys accompanied her son to school every morning until she realized that the practice wasn't quite as acceptable in a big city as in a tiny town.

Actually Vernon went with Elvis the first day,

confident he had left the boy in safe hands. An hour or so later he was surprised to find Elvis back home. It was all too much for him. The school building itself was awesome, bigger than anything he'd ever seen. He feared getting lost in it. As for the hundreds of other students in the school, they were too many for him to cope with. Elvis didn't wait to find out; he was convinced they'd make fun of him.

Elvis returned to school the next day. He made his way slowly through the maze of corridors of the physical building and through the complexities of understanding the new young people he would have to get along with for two years.

Of course, he was right in fearing he'd be made fun of. Kids who are different always are and besides being a backwoods kid, there was Elvis' stubborn, inexplicable refusal to become one of the crowd. Certainly he had no intention of looking like them.

So at the outset Elvis was labelled "freaky" and as soon as their former schoolmate became famous, stories proliferated about his time at Hume. Some may stray from the truth but, in essence, they picture an oddball newcomer entering a world entirely different to him, anxious to be liked but really not especially concerned if people responded to him. Elvis was quite at home in his own company, with his guitar, his songs, his own way of life.

This is not to infer that Elvis retired to some corner of the building to sit and sulk. He made quite a few friends. He was a husky one hundred and seventy pounds and played football for at least one year with the school team. As the kids grew to know him they inevitably came to understand him better.

The things Elvis had going for him were his singing and his guitar. In a sense, he was a Pied Piper, a young troubadour. When it got around how well Elvis sang, they'd gather and ask him to perform. Elvis was neither reticent or aggressive about his "parlor entertaining." However, once he started, he gave it all he had. And the kids' respect and appreciation began to grow. Eventually Elvis' personality was established enough that it was taken for granted and they called him "the kid with the sideburns," letting it go at that.

But it hadn't been easy. Elvis' refusal to cut his hair or shave his sideburns led to more than one fist fight. Some, Elvis won on his own. But to hear the stories told today, for a kid with a reputation as a "loner," Elvis literally had hundreds of "friends" who pitched in and helped when he needed it.

Tupelo had a reputation as a well-integrated town for its era. In Memphis, Elvis found friends among blacks. This met with expected taunts by white students at Hume, and the usual racial slurs. Elvis' hecklers found him quick to anger on this point, quicker with his fists. One story has it that he pushed his hand through a window to grab one boy by the collar, holding him there while he smashed his face with his free hand.

Still, a few accounts like these hardly compose a picture of Elvis as a gregarious, *hail-fellow, well-met* student, the automatic choice for President of the Student Body and any other office that happened to be lying about. He'd made progress in getting along with the "new world" of Memphis, but Elvis still remained a "loner," finding deep satisfaction within himself, searching for the elusive intangible—would he ever know it or recognize it when it appeared?—that would lead him where he hoped he belonged—in the world of music.

*   *   *

He explored Memphis hungrily, drinking in everything that it offered. He heard the music coming out of the saloons along Beale Street and he discovered how different it was from the stuff he was singing. The songs were rhythmic, sexier than the standards; crude, perhaps, to a more sophisticated ear. To Elvis, they were exciting. Gradually the black rhythms began to show in his own singing.

Subconsciously Elvis was developing a dual personality. There were his good manners in company, his quiet efforts to get along at school despite some fights, his obvious shyness. But once the music started, the costume on his back, and the rhythms began to pound, Elvis was a different personality—a strutting, swaggering, swivel-hipped bundle of energy that would become Presley, the star.

*   *   *

Elvis realized he had to help out his family, so he began reaching for part-time, after-school jobs. He ushered briefly at a theatre until he got into a fistfight about the usual thing—his long hair and sideburns. He was somewhat more successful at mowing lawns, hanging around neighborhoods at the time the man of the house came home. He made his pitch for the job, and he was rolling along fine with his side-lines until they got out of hand. Elvis was so tired that he began falling asleep in class.

Elvis still respected his mother. She'd talked him out of playing football, fearing injury. Now she made him quit some of his jobs, and went to work herself at a hospital.

However bleak or unpromising their situation, Elvis came first. It may sound like molly-coddling but digging deeper into the philosophy of the Presleys, one finds their parental behavior no different from that of the immigrants who filled the big cities, working long, hard hours at low pay, making awesome sacrifices for the benefit of their children.

Vernon and Gladys Presley were, by no means, old parents; old in years or in attitudes. But they recognized their limitations. Neither was well-enough educated to improve their situation. Vernon's health would only survive hard work for a given number of years. How much wiser to do what they could for their boy?

Elvis was just an average student. He knew it and so did his parents. He was a country kid where scholars indeed existed but they weren't exactly as common as horseflies. Elvis hadn't enjoyed the educational advantages of the city children. He was lucky to be holding his own.

So whenever Elvis earned a few dollars or there was extra money in the till, he sallied forth to Beale Street to buy the hot pink shirts, studded belts, yellow trousers he favored. With his long hair in contrast to the short style of other young men, Elvis often looked like a sinister imitation of an old silent movie villain. When you added his colorful clothes to his dark Latin looks, the resemblance was startling.

Whether they admitted it or not, the girls at Hume were fascinated by Elvis. As a teenager he was already exuding the sex appeal that made teeny-boppers swoon a few years later. Even when they joined in the jokes poking fun at his appearance, they weren't exactly uninterested when Elvis asked them for a date. Those who weren't on Elvis' list resorted to the usual expression of scorn, "A nice girl wouldn't be seen with someone like Elvis Presley."

That was the big surprise. Often when parents opened the door to greet Elvis who'd arrived to pick up his date, they'd gasp at his outrageous get-up. A few seconds later they were overwhelmed by the charm of this devastating young man with manners that could have been learned at Buckingham Palace instead of in the backwoods home of two poor farm people.

He spoke softly and quietly, addressing his seniors as "Ma'am" and "Sir," never missed a "thank you" or "please", and treated his young lady with the courtliness one expected of a young gentleman born and reared on an elegant, graceful Southern plantation.

There was one special girl in Elvis' life whom he started courting when they were in high school. It was quite a love affair—accounting for a major change in Elvis' life. He spent hours hidden in the bushes waiting for a glimpse of her, jealous because she'd gone out with someone else. He was persistent, but the girl, although she liked him enormously, wasn't quite sure that Elvis was her style.

Gladys was the first to recognize that theirs was more than an ordinary case of puppy love. Vernon brushed it off, saying that it was time for Elvis to be interested in girls and he was just beginning to discover it.

Reports don't quite jibe as to who terminated the infatuation. It appears fairly clear that the girl eventually changed her mind about Elvis and fell in love with him. But it was too late, at least in the light of her own reaction to the situation.

Elvis, after graduation, didn't become an over-night smash in show business, but he began working at a job and singing around at road houses and night clubs. This kept him on the run, and now it was the girl who looked out the window at the bushes to see when Elvis got home. They had gone so far as to become secretly engaged, waiting for graduation and a more propitious time to make it public.

Whatever, the girl married Elvis' more serious rival and for a time he seemed to show no interest in girls or in that busy occupation of young people, searching for someone to go steady with.

Elvis' last year in high school was the busiest and perhaps the happiest he had spent in Memphis. Elvis was Elvis. Everybody could see him coming a mile away but there were no more snide remarks. They were eager to have him around. Elvis was the kid who'd brightened their picnics with his guitar, his songs and the frantic movements of his body. He'd become, in the language of the times, "hot stuff."

Elvis appeared in one of Hume's variety shows and, according to the rules, the performer who got the most applause was allowed to sing an encore. This was Elvis' first brush with "professionalism." He went on, did his singing and came off to whistles, cheers and stomping of feet. "He was so surprised," said his teacher, "that he couldn't believe it. He kept saying over and over, 'They like me! They like me!'"

At his high school graduation, Elvis sang before his first big audience, sixteen hundred people.

They were a preview of audiences to come. They cheered. They whistled. They wanted more—and Elvis was permitted a fast encore.

It had to have been a triumph for the kid from Tupelo who, a few years earlier, had run back home, terrified by the hugeness of the school building, fearful of being among so many people. Now he was singing to a huge auditorium—packed to the hilt—sixteen hundred people!

It was his first taste of the excitement he could generate in an audience. An excitement that never diminished as Elvis switched from a battered old Plymouth to the second-hand cars of his high school years and finally his private fleet of white Cadillacs as he sang, strummed and wiggled his way to superstardom.

33

*   *   *

Elvis knew little about Show Business—beyond what he found in the movies, on television or heard on the radio. And in the late forties it was pretty sorry stuff. When Elvis graduated from high school, he got a variety of jobs, the most natural one for him being a truck driver. He fit the build and his appearance seemed more at home as one of the "men of the road"—fellows who, like himself, were rugged individualists, even if they were never quite sure why.

As for the entertainment business Elvis was shortly to embrace, it was in pretty bad shape. True, there was early TV with its live dramatic shows where sets collapsed around the actors, new stars like Imogene Coca and Sid Caesar.

A few years later, Milton Berle would join other old-timers in accepting the new medium. Ed Wynn, Jack Benny, Burns and Allen, Eddie Cantor would all move over from the serenity of radio studios to the frenetic world of sound stages, cables, sound trucks, cameras, improvised dressing rooms, blackboards—the lot. It was depressing—like shuffling old uncles and grandfathers around in a chess game.

Hollywood had enjoyed incredible success during the war with movies that mixed the old patriotic hokum with sheer nonsense like musicals starring Doris Day, the Andrews Sisters, comedians Abbott and Costello, Judy Garland, Mickey Rooney, and sturdy great ladies: Joan Crawford, Bette Davis,

Claudette Colbert, Vivien Leigh, Greer Garson and numerous others. The big male stars had gone to war—Clark Gable, James Stewart, Henry Fonda, Tyrone Power—leaving older players like Humphrey Bogart, Paul Henreid and Spencer Tracy to suddenly loom as romantic figures.

As one disgruntled Hollywood writer described America's wartime movies: "Men love God, men love country, men love machinery, men love men, men no longer love women."

For young people of Elvis' age, there was nothing original coming along. Hollywood, bloated by wartime profits, felt threatened by television, and was holding back waiting to judge the market. They were horrified when along came the neo-realism of the Italian cinema, the first successful example being *Bicycle Thief*.

The film tycoons remembered only a sequence of the masterpiece showing a kid "pissing in the streets." They moaned, "You can't tell me this is what the public wants."

Perhaps not. Surely not as a steady diet. But they were eager to react to something—or some person—closer to their own age, who felt their restlessness more than keenly than Doris Day and her "awfully nice" records.

There was Marlon Brando, of course, who first set the Broadway stage agog with his superb, animal-like performance in Tennessee Williams' *A Streetcar Named Desire*, a role he performed later on the screen. Moody James Dean was standing in the wings waiting to take his turn at capturing the rebellious spirit of the young people of the era, kids who had never really understood World War II and now that it was over were bored to death.

If they were too young to understand the war, they now were old enough to realize that the war had forever smashed old values, particularly the culture and life style of their parents. It was time for a change—and the kids had no intention of waiting for the politicians to tell them what they already knew. History had taught them some things—the establishment is hard to budge, but it is not immoveable if the force of numbers is behind it.

Had teenagers before ever created their own culture, their special, individualistic life style? Not in these United States. But they were about to, and the odd-looking kid from Memphis with the duck tail, the pink shirt, the touch of acne on his face—the surly guy—was on the threshold of answering their dissatisfaction.

*   *   *

Elvis obviously was not college material, so he decided to study a trade. He began working as a truck driver for the Crown Electric Company while studying for a career as an electrician. He had been at the job a few months when his mother's birthday came along.

He decided to give her a very special present—a record. It cost four dollars and it took only a few minutes to make. Elvis knew exactly where to go, the Memphis Recording Studio, a store front he'd passed many times. It was a sideline operation of the Sun Record Company, owned by Sam Phillips.

Neither operation was what could be called a smashing financial success, but they made enough profit to keep Sam going. The Memphis Recording Studio was the place where kids went to record messages to their parents, where whole families gathered to speak self-conscious greetings to grandparents on Golden Wedding anniversaries and the like.

Make Your Own Record establishments had been around a long time, usually hidden upstairs in office buildings. They didn't appear on the streets in store fronts until World War II when the home-made record became a favored form of communication between servicemen and their families.

The woman in charge of the shop the day Elvis showed up with his four dollars, guitar, and in his spectacular wardrobe was Marion Keisker, a friendly, well-known woman in her thirties who had enjoyed a long career in radio. She had only recently retired as "Miss Radio of Memphis" to serve as Sam's office manager.

Marion Keisker has been obliged to tell the story many times. According to her, Elvis came in and, since it was a busy afternoon, she asked him to wait his turn. He sat down politely and quietly as usual. Marion engaged him in conversation. She asked him what kind of singer he was—a question that evidently confused young Elvis who finally figured he'd satisfy her curiosity by saying, "I don't sound like nobody."

The Ink Spots were among Elvis' favorite singers, and he chose *My Happiness* for the first song and *That's When Your Heartaches Began* for the second. Elvis accompanied himself on the guitar and went through the two numbers with considerable aplomb, considering that *Your Heartaches* was one of those weepy ballads with recitation tucked in between the choruses. Later Elvis described the recording as sounding like "somebody beating on a bucket lid."

As Elvis was singing the first number, Marion knew there was someone standing in front of her who spelled *personality* to her well-trained ear. She decided to tape the song, but could only find a short piece of crumpled tape to work with. Rather than taking a chance on missing out, she used it. "Now, this is something we never did," she said. "But I wanted Sam Phillips to hear it. I don't think even Elvis knew that I was taping it."

Sam Phillips had been around Memphis radio for years. Weary of the same old programming forced on him by station policy, he decided to go into business for himself, setting up his own professional recording and distribution company as well as the store front operation to help pay the freight.

Sam had strong feelings about black music. He liked it. He felt its vitality and complained that prejudice prevented great black artists from being heard. He recorded some of Memphis' finest singers, Bobby Bland, Jackie Brenston, Chester (The Howlin' Wolf) Burnett and Doc Ross. He also recorded Joe Hill Louis, B.B. King and Big Walter Horton. He was the first ever to record these artists.

Time and time again he told friends and associates in the business, "It seems to me that Negroes are the only ones who have any freshness left in their music. If I could find a white man who had the Negro sound and the Negro feel, I could make a billion dollars."

This was the quality Marion Keisker found in Elvis. Sam Phillips heard the tape and filed Presley's name in his memory vault. He told Marion, "You're right. But he needs a lot of work."

In the months that followed Elvis came back a couple of times to make records on his own. He met Sam and that helped because it gave Phillips a mental picture of what Marion described as "the boy with sideburns." Elvis nearly joined a family group, the Blackwoods, when a member considered quitting then decided to stay on. Although obviously disappointed, he stayed friendly with the Blackwoods, singing with them at tent revivals and church gatherings.

But the pot of gold, Elvis and Marion suspected, lay in landing a record with Sam Phillips. Maybe Sam suspected this too, but no one came right out and said so. Every time a record came up, Marion suggested it for Elvis, but Sam, intuitively perhaps, wiggled out of a commitment. He was waiting for the right song.

Finally, Sam Phillips found something he thought suitable for Elvis. Elvis was second choice. Sam had gotten hold of a dub record and would have preferred to release it as it came to him. But Sam couldn't find out who the original singer was so he decided to give Elvis a try.

"It was a Saturday afternoon," Sam said later, "and it was like that old story of calling the actor, turning around to open the door to see a young man standing there, saying, 'Here I am, Mr. De Mille.' Elvis must have run all the way."

The song was *Without Love There is Nothing*. He called musicians Scotty Moore and Bill Black to meet Elvis, hoping they could work together.

Phillips introduced them. After hours of trying this style and that, nothing jelled. *Without Love* simply didn't come off, although Elvis recorded it as a single fifteen years later.

In spite of the disappointment of their first effort, the three young men kept on trying, not for days or weeks but several months. They worked at night clubs and Elvis was beginning to enjoy quite a reputation as an entertainer around Memphis. Because he was forced—and willing—to work for peanuts, he held on to his job with the electric company.

It took months of trying out various materials at Sam's studio before the *Elvis Sound* finally exploded.

It happened during one of the boys' numerous jam sessions. Out of sheer frustration, Elvis let go and bellowed the lyrics with extraordinary fervor. He began clowning, rocking, jumping and pulsating with the beat of the song. It was contagious. Scotty and Bill joined in.

The recording of *That's All Right Mama* was originally sung by Big Boy Grudup, a black country singer, who Elvis said had been one of his influences.

Choosing something for the flip side took just as much effort if not quite as long. Finally they worked out a version of *Blue Moon of Kentucky* which would please the more traditional country music listeners.

Sam Phillips took the record—a strange mixture of sensual black field jazz and plaintive country music rhythm—to disc jockey Dewey Phillips, who played it on his radio program. A minute after the record was played the phones began ringing and everyone wanted to know who the singer was. Dewey called Sam and told him to get hold of Elvis. They found him hiding out in a movie theatre, afraid that everyone would laugh at him.

Elvis high-tailed it to the radio station where he sat down and talked to Dewey for about half an hour, telling all about himself, where he came from, where he'd gone to school, answering questions with that quiet politeness of his. Finally he asked, "Mr. Phillips, when are we going on the air?" Dewey laughed, "Son, you've been on the air all this time. This mike's been open."

Elvis turned pale and virtually fainted. It was his very first radio interview but the result was fantastic. Seven thousand copies of the record were sold in Memphis alone. Elvis signed with Bob Neal for a barnstorming tour of Texas, Arkansas and Louisiana. Elvis' draped jackets, pegged pants, spectacular sports shirts, his mop of brilliantined hair, sideburns, his boudoir eyes and his bumps and grinds had an explosive effect on bobby soxers. Elvis was beginning to be more than a local sensation.

*   *   *

Orders for the record poured in at such a rate that the Sun Company had trouble filling them. While it was a triumph for the small record company, Elvis' career was just beginning. No one realized this more keenly than Presley.

He'd been around Memphis enough to know that a performer's career represented long, hard work. He hadn't found his first hit overnight. It had been the result of long, hard and dedicated effort.

Moreover, while *That's All Right Mama* may rightfully be considered Elvis Presley's first hit, its career was mercurial. It sold about twenty thousand copies which was good for a regional record. *Billboard*, the bible of the record business, reviewed it by saying: *(Elvis Presley) is a potent new chanter who can sock out a tune either for the country or the r&p markets.*

Chapter 3

What had happened in the Memphis studio was historic musically. In cutting the two discs, Elvis and his backup men had achieved a blend of white country music and black blues. As innovative as it sounds today, the combination was not welcomed everywhere in the country.

Elvis' first record became a hit in the regional sense but numerous disc jockeys refused to play it because they thought Elvis was just another black singer. Or what was worse in the eyes of both races, a white singer trying to sing "black." There were many of these around in the fifties when the record business began to flourish—names that blossomed briefly and were seldom heard from again.

They sent out thousands of copies of the record but as soon as disc jockeys saw the *Blue Moon of Kentucky* on the label they tossed it out as "another bluegrass number." Some stations told Sam Phillips that Elvis was too country for them; others complained that he was too *black*.

But it did serve an immediate Presley need. He was able to collect a few hundred dollars as the return came in, and from the record there came appearances on Nashville's *Grand Ole Opry* and Shreveport's *Louisiana Hayride*.

Nabbing *Grand Ole Opry* after only one record was the first major Presley accomplishment. This long-established radio show represented the heights to country singers, and one seldom ever got close to it until stardom had been a matter of years, not just a few weeks.

Grand Ole Opry wasn't quite the hit Elvis hoped for. The producer expected a bigger band than Scotty and Bill. Their ability to create a big sound didn't occur to him. Why should it? They'd done a pretty remarkable thing. Still, when the performance was over, the man unkindly told Elvis he ought to go back to driving a truck.

That was an unexpected and unnecessary slur and Elvis took it with little grace. He wasn't ready for jibes at this early stage of the game and cried all the way home. The Shreveport show, *Hayride*, turned out better. He was treated sympathetically and enthusiastically by the producers there—performing so well that in the next year Elvis was invited back so many times it appeared that he'd become a regular attraction.

Marion Keisker often told the story of Elvis' first appearance before a huge audience, when he was booked in an all-country show at the Overton Park Shell.

Marion asked a woman standing next to her, "Who have you come to see?"

"Marty Robbins. I never miss him. Who did you come to see?"

"Elvis Presley."

"Never heard of him. Who's he?"

"After this show, you won't ask me," Marion replied.

According to some sources there was a bit of a hassle because Sam's recording company wasn't unionized and Elvis had not signed up with any of the theatrical unions, never really having played a union situation.

But that doesn't make sense. To have appeared on *Grand Ole Opry* and *Hayride* Elvis must have joined AGVA *(American Guild of Variety Artists)*, but perhaps some local union situation was involved.

Whatever, the money was scraped up for Elvis' initiation fee. Elvis went on stage and shook the platform with *Good Rockin' Tonight* and left the platform with the audience screaming and bellowing its approval.

Elvis had passed an acid test—pleasing a big crowd who knew their entertainers and could tell the difference between a genuine star performer and an up and coming newcomer. They placed Elvis where he belonged—a star.

In October, 1954, just two months after *That's All Right* made its debut, Elvis' *Good Rockin' Tonight* was released. It was followed in 1955 by three more successes, *Milkcow Blues Boogie, I'm Left, You're Right, She's Gone* and *Mystery Train*.

Elvis was earning big money but his popularity

remained regional. He was voted "the most promising new country performer of the year" by *Billboard* magazine, one of many national trade magazines to climb aboard the Presley bandwagon.

Billboard had given him his first encouragement, and now the magazine was coming through again. In its first review, it suggested Elvis' versatility—that he was acceptable in both the "blues" and the "pop" market.

This gave Elvis the idea that he could do anything he happened to like—whatever was popular on the juke box at the time. Sam Phillips knew better. He realized young Elvis had the beginning of a style of his own; the sort of music that interested him. That was his old complaint—the record industry's reluctance to innovate—and what had led him into organizing his own business in the first place.

Sam had to persuade Elvis to tackle new stuff. It wasn't easy for, unlike most artists who recorded for Sun, Elvis didn't write his material. Songs had to be literally written on the spot.

This was the pattern of his career. Nothing came easily. Elvis discovered early in the game that the answer to success lay in hard work, trial and error. He disliked rehearsing. But Sam and Miriam were old show-wise hands. They made him sit down and do it their way. For Elvis, it turned out the right way.

In July, 1954, Elvis signed a contract with disc jockey Bob Neal.

The first time Elvis went on the road he was part of a group, put together by Neal with the d.j. acting as master of ceremonies. Elvis, Scotty and Bill were billed as the *Blue Moon Boys*. They moved around in a battered car, playing dates wherever they could find them. The pay was poor but it gradually increased to the point where they could command three hundred dollars a night. Still, it was nip and tuck all the way—considering the expenses involved in driving and housing and feeding three young men.

Neal's radio radius extended about two hundred miles, but word-of-mouth eventually enlarged their range and for bookings further away from Memphis they were able to ask four hundred dollars.

*   *   *

The thrill of discovery is a privilege the public reserves for itself, yet the producer or promoter who later takes credit for "creating a star" may be entitled to his little boasts. Giving fresh talent opportunity has been his privilege and good fortune. But the people ultimately make up their mind whether or not his choice has been a wise one.

Robert Taylor, for example, was brought to Hollywood with the improbable name of Spangler Arlington Brugh from the mid-west with little experience in acting beyond amateur and semi-professional work. He was signed to a contract on the strength of his looks, an attractive personality and a solid baritone voice that could read from the beginning of a simple declarative sentence to the end.

The studio threw him into a bit part, playing a doctor in a secondary feature, *Society Doctor*.

Within two weeks of its New York opening Taylor's name was up in lights. Word-of-mouth advertising about "the beautiful young man" spread so fast that second-run theatres where the movie was playing suddenly found lines waiting at the boxoffice, a rare experience for them in the grim depression year of 1935, the one in which Elvis Presley was born. Metro-Goldwyn-Mayer may have made it possible, but the fans *discovered* Robert Taylor.

One of the more exciting theatrical events of the fifties was the initial meshing of Elvis Presley and people. He was still largely unheard-of outside the south. And the solution lay in the tri-state tour conceived by Bob Neal and eventually enlarged to include the entire country, when Colonel Parker took over Elvis' contract.

Money, so scarce before, suddenly began to pour in. His first big purchase was a pink Cadillac. His second was a lavish forty thousand dollar home which he bought in a smart Memphis residential neighborhood. Graceland came along later.

The tours taught Elvis his trade. Elvis had been heard so often on radio that he was already a warm, old friend. Now audiences were given an opportunity to meet him. So Elvis got behind the wheel of his pink Cadillac and started off with just an average entourage.

If there were worries about how the tour was going to turn out, they were wasted. It was amazing. A show business phenomenon. Before tickets went on sale, even before Vernon and Gladys Presley had taken possession of their new ranch house in the best part of Memphis, the tour was stamped a success.

From small auditoriums to large ball parks, *Elvis Presley—In Person* sold out. Girls formed the largest part of his audience, flocking to see him. His fans were multiplying like rabbits and perceptive commentators of the music scene realized Elvis represented exactly what the teenagers of the fifties were looking for—an idol who could bring some excitement and vitality into their humdrum lives.

Schoolhouse shows were a tradition in the south. Elvis later recalled that when he was travelling with Neal they'd drive to the location, set up their equipment and there wouldn't be a car in sight. Suddenly, out of nowhere, a whole audience appeared. At first Bob Neal was the attraction of the tour, although they'd certainly come to hear Presley too. But eventually it was Presley who created the boxoffice stir, the kid who sold the tickets.

The incredible success Elvis met signalled that it was time to change from tickets spun off a roll into hard tickets—the kind you find in stadiums, the legitimate theatre and concert halls; pasteboards and ducats in the vernacular. The kind of tickets the late Mike Todd had the greatest respect for. He'd work as hard at building an advance sale as producing a show. When he counted the advance take at the end of a day, Mike would smile and say, "I never heard of anyone going broke collecting money."

*   *   *

The Sunbelt may appear to be the discovery of Wall Street investors of the 1970's, of industry searching for better living conditions, less expensive labor, and of northerners weary of the long, cold winter, frightened by the dreadful warnings of scientists who have predicted worse winters to come. Obviously, these dire phophecies are intended to distract us from the scientists' dismal failure to float California out to sea as it was supposed to several years ago.

Whatever, the *Sunbelt* is now "very much the 'in' place" in finance, society, industry, the resort business, replacing for middle-America the California of the 1930's where the saying went, "If heaven is anything like here, I sure want to go there."

There is a drawback. Like the northeast, *The Sunbelt* lives with "weather," unlike California which boasts of "climate." But Madison Avenue will come up with something and the *Sunbelt* ultimately will have its own *Sunbeltese*, and we will mourn the gracious language of the south and the softness of its accents.

The preceding paragraphs are typical of what any good newspaperman would shudder at as a rambling lead and a long way to the point that the *Sunbelt* is old, old hat to seldom-heard-of Show Biz entrepreneurs who grew rich and fat on its wonderful audiences long before Elvis Presley and even when the estimable Colonel Thomas Parker was in kneepants.

Long before radio, producers could send the equivalent of today's truck and bus shows into the

South and Southwest in anything from *Peg 'O My Heart* to *Uncle Tom's Cabin*, assured that they would produce pure gold. Stars of the era enjoyed playing the South because of the warm hospitality they received, plus full, attentive, intelligent audiences. Any Victor Herbert operetta touring in the twenties could fill the same auditoriums that Elvis appeared in during the fifties.

The arrangements were no different then than Elvis found them. There wouldn't be a soul in sight until the performers arrived. Then, out of nowhere, whole communities of people would appear to see the show and afterward to drink and celebrate with the actors long into the night.

Cartoon shows were popular—*Mutt and Jeff, Maggie and Jiggs, Bringing Up Father, Tillie the Toiler*. Producers bundled a few skilled comics, a couple of singers and dancers into cars, threw a band into a station wagon, some props and scenery into a truck—and off they'd go. From Hagerstown, Maryland, down to the small towns of Louisiana, along the Gulf to the Texas panhandle, through Arizona, New Mexico and the tip of California, they could count on full houses for a night or two.

They were careful to avoid the big cities where some *smart-ass* critic might review the production. Or worse, a lawyer representing the cartoon's creator might catch up with a show and obtain a "cease and desist" court order to prevent further exploitation of the title and characters.

For the troupers it only amounted to a temporary inconvenience. They simply switched titles. *Maggie and Jiggs* and *Mutt and Jeff* were interchangeable. Eventually the cartoons' authors decided prosecution and court orders were worthless. Anyhow, when the Depression came along, it meant throwing actors out of work. *Sunbelt* audiences had thinned out like those in the rest of the country.

Regional entertainers made fortunes in the *Sunbelt* for the same reason that Elvis Presley was able to begin his career there so auspiciously. Southerners place a premium on their culture, particularly their musical inheritance, both black and white. In the theatrical history of America, this same loyalty is seldom found elsewhere. States have their pageant spectacles—like California's *Ramona*, but they are occasional events rather than continuing celebrations like the *Grand Ole Opry* radio show, virtually a half century old.

*　　*　　*

Colonel Thomas A. Parker prefers to leave a lot about himself to the imagination—including the details of his origin. He will not argue that he was born in West Virginia in 1910, or that he was a member of the Parker family which at the time was operating a carnival in the *Sunbelt*. Since his parents were performers too, young Tom became one himself, working animal acts.

But his talents lay outside the circus tent where he served best as a spieler for the show, an enterprising barker who would promise "admission free with every paid ticket." Parker's military title is purely honorary, but a "Colonel" was commonplace—and expected—in the circus world. Anyone with Parker's distinguished appearance, bald pate, broad-brimmed hat, a wide stomach covered with a watch chain and an expensive cigar in his hand, was entitled to be called "Colonel."

Parker's talents were many and varied. He invented the foot-long hot dog—so legend has it. He also worked in off-season as a dogcatcher in Tampa and applied showmanship to this unlikeable trade. He found homes for all unclaimed puppies, although it probably cost him most of his salary to do it.

But the Colonel, in those days or now, was not one to worry about money. He struck a hard bargain when the opportunity was there. He'd accept a few bills and change when it wasn't. Colonel Parker rode with the times. His star rose in the *Sunbelt* as the man who could promote anything from a County Fair to stars like Gene Austin, Eddy Arnold and Hank Snow.

It has often been said that 1955 was the year of Elvis. But it is equally true that it was also the year of Colonel Tom Parker. Like any true promoter, from Barnum to Mike Todd, from Billy Minsky to Billy Rose, there is that longing for that one big piece of pie—the act that is going to soar from peanuts to millions.

It's like the story of the concession man who used to go to sleep dreaming that one night the microphone would be all his at the Hollywood Bowl and he would be given exactly one minute to pitch binoculars. "Then I'd retire."

Parker's genial, outgoing personality masked a shrewd bargainer of whom it was often said, "You'll make money with Colonel Parker; that is, if you don't drop dead from his terms."

Elvis was growing too big as a recording star for Sun Records and too successful an attraction for Bob Neal to handle. Neal, devoted to his wife and family, was a personality in his own right. There simply wasn't time for him to tour with Elvis.

For Elvis, the transition was smooth, although there had been some preliminary skirmishes in his managerial department. But they hadn't affected Neal or Sam Phillips. RCA bought out Sun Records—a move which brought Presley into the big time record-wise. Colonel Tom Parker became Elvis' personal manager.

Neither name meant much to the titans of theatrical industry, the big agents in New York and Hollywood, who were supposed to be on top of everything, companies whose stationery featured office addresses and representatives around the world. But in 1956 they weren't writing about the *Sunbelt* on the drama pages of *The New York Times*.

Even George Burns couldn't get a laugh wondering if the name came from the infamous *Gus Sun Time* of his vaudeville days. It was the roughest of all the circuits where acts played as many shows as the local manager wanted and jumped from town to town like jack rabbits, but it possessed unassailable virtues; the pay was good and the management totally responsible. A Gus Sun contract amounted to money in the bank.

So management of the century's biggest money making entertainer passed into the hands of the *Sunbelt's* Colonel Parker, then forty-five. Elvis was twenty-one.

*   *   *

Landing Elvis gave the Colonel a second wind. He needed it to keep up with his youthful star who, although he never drank, sometimes got so caught up in his enthusiasms and excitement that one would swear he was drunk. The Colonel had his hands full keeping him in line. He was careful not to let Elvis make too many moves on his own.

The veteran showman had his skills—handling performers was one of them. They were all difficult, temperamental, easily hurt. Whether carnival strong men, circus acrobats, or country singers like Elvis.

The Colonel wasn't exactly sure what kind of singer Elvis was when they teamed up. But he didn't have to think twice to realize Elvis was someone very special indeed who could cause such a commotion in an audience that Hank Snow had been jolted by the idea of having to follow him.

The Colonel had the imagination to sense that the source of Elvis' appeal lay in his movements—that in his shimmy, revolving hips, rolling pelvis, he was actually performing a strip tease. "Female entertainers had been doing it for years," the Colonel said, "Elvis did it in reverse."

Parker played his cards right and the new year

was opened with a bang. In January, 1956, Elvis' recording of *Heartbreak Hotel* was released. The single immediately jumped to the number one spot on the national charts and sold over a million copies throughout the United States.

It was Elvis' first gold record. He had jumped the Mason-Dixon line to become a national headliner. He was not just a "country singer" charming the South. Some months earlier Elvis had travelled to New York to audition for Arthur Godfrey's TV *Talent Show*. He was rejected, but the Colonel told him not to worry, that in time, all the national shows would be begging for him—and they'd have to pay big money. As the Colonel put it, "top coin."

They did. First, RCA pressed five of Sun's unreleased records Presley had made and they caught on immediately. Teenagers went wild. His old records were repressed and they too joined the ranks of big sellers. Presley was the hottest new entertainer of the decade—and you had to go back before the war to find someone his equal in instantaneous appeal. That would have to be Sinatra—which certainly was going way, way back.

Television was where the money and promotion potential could be found. No one knew this more keenly than the Colonel. What no one expected was the furor Elvis' initial television appearance created. From the tone of newspapers of the day, front page, editorials, columns, one would assume that a national crisis had been created by the sweet-looking young man who wiggled his hips as he sang. It was almost as though the Republic itself was in danger.

Elvis wasn't happy. He was too young and too new in the business to adjust to such rough criticism. It took him time and all of Colonel Parker's fatherly persuasiveness before common sense overcame his sensibilities.

But Colonel Parker knew he'd found his big piece of pie in the sky.

Chapter 4

"I don't want him on my show. I don't care what anyone says about him—how great a talent he is—he just won't be in my show and that's that."

The words came from Ed Sullivan, one of television's curious creations, an absolutely untalented individual, whose nickname *The Great Stoneface* derived from the fact that Ed Sullivan, amused, looked no different from Ed Sullivan in deepest despair. Yet for years Ed Sullivan's *Toast of the Town*, later to be called the *Ed Sullivan Show*, dominated television's variety entertainment with unflagging energy, maintaining a strong rating year after year almost until the end of its existence.

Sullivan came to his eminence as a television personality, producer and master of ceremonies by way of a long career of newspapering. He was a columnist for the New York *Daily News*, the city's biggest tabloid and claimant to the largest circulation of any newspaper in America.

Originally a sports writer, Sullivan moved over to the entertainment pages as the rage for gossip flourished in the twenties much as it does today. He ran a poor second to Walter Winchell's skill as a collector of *exclusives* and had none of Winchell's style as a writer and phrase-maker.

The News, however, found a unique niche for Sullivan as the paper's public relations personality. The paper staged a number of events in the course of the year, the *Golden Gloves* tournament to promote young boxers and *The Harvest Moon Ball*, a dancing contest which he supervised to huge audiences at Madison Square Garden.

Once or twice a year Sullivan took over the stage of one of the Broadway theatres, usually Loew's State, to present the dancers, winners of various contests, a couple of standard acts and celebrities who needed the good will they found in his column.

The movie stars did what they could. The Hollywood people simply came on and said "hello." The variety artists, perhaps, sang or danced. They amounted to an "extra added attraction" to the top heavy entertainment programs of the era—a feature movie, newsreel, short feature, organ recital and a variety show.

When TV became competitive, Sullivan's name came up for a show in the assumption that he would be able to produce big name talent, using the pressure of his column. In this respect, the network was right but, to their surprise, Sullivan became a personality himself, mimicked, made fun of, held in low esteem by entertainers like Milton Berle and Steve Allen who headed their own variety shows. Unlike Stoneface their talents were broader than mispronouncing the names of operatic arias and stumbling over simple English words.

But Sullivan became a canny producer and eventually he ruled his show with an iron hand, making it a unique springboard for new talent and a haven for old-timers who needed to remind the public they were still around, as well as the money Sullivan paid.

To his credit he didn't use his newspaper connection as a bargaining point. By the time the show was rolling, standard salaries had been established in all categories and no one argued them. Sullivan was highly regarded by the stars and acts who worked his show, even if they cursed him roundly for cutting their routines, holding some of the biggest names down to four and five minutes. It was a terribly difficult show for some performers to play, but Sullivan encountered few rejections.

He'd accomplished some hair-raising boo-boos, like inviting the public to write him whether it was "right and proper" for Ingrid Bergman to appear on his program in view of her scandalous liaison with director Roberto Rossellini and the birth of their illegitimate twins. The vote was overwhelmingly in favor of Miss Bergman and Sullivan, red-faced, humbly admitted he'd made a stupid blunder.

Sullivan might have made a worse gaffe had he not been showman enough to realize that Elvis Presley was the hottest new property in the entertainment business and would make it on TV— with or without Ed Sullivan's Sunday night showcase.

Elvis' reputation as a sex symbol made waves in

TV circles. To TV bigwigs, he meant ratings, ratings meant money and that was reason enough to put him on the air. To Colonel Parker it meant big money too, and that was reason enough for Elvis to agree to appear.

But Elvis gyrating on the TV screen brought up questions of taste. The home screen was different from performing on stages and auditoriums in the South. Presley's image emerged as a contradiction too complex for television's sponsors and producers to understand. He had the looks of a hoodlum; yet, he talked like a saint.

On-stage he was a maniac, pouting, swiveling, wiggling, curling his lips, using the microphone as a sensual object, an extention of himself. His style was totally wild, primitive and audiences reacted to it with shrieks, moans and groans, as though they were caught up in the ecstasy of sex. Girls screamed and swooned.

It was a throwback to the Sinatra days—but much more complicated—like the times. Presley brought a new dimension to popular entertainment. It wasn't half a style but a complete one. Elvis Presley was the star who invented himself. His influence on the personal and entertainment tastes of teenagers grew with lightning speed. It opened the door for almost every new teenage craze that has come along in the ensuing years.

The same young men who made fun of girls who sighed over Presley began letting their own hair grow. They created a demand for stylists—not barbers. As a high school kid, Elvis saved his pennies to have his styled and dressed in a woman's beauty parlor.

Elvis not only set the music world on fire, he shook up the whole record business. Soon it had to be admitted that Elvis Presley was changing the whole shape of American pop music.

Elvis tried to explain his style; "I don't know what happens to me when I sing. Maybe it's the music, the song, the crowd or something deep inside me. The rock 'n' roll beat gets me. I have to move my hands, feet, knees, legs, my head—everything. There were attacks on my singing style in the paper. I felt I could live them down."

The first of Elvis' televised performances coincided with the release of *Heartbreak Hotel*. It was introduced on the Dorsey Brothers Saturday night program, *Stage Show*, aired on CBS. The battle between the networks had begun.

The show was telecast on January 28th, 1956 and Elvis was paid one thousand, two hundred fifty dollars. The Dorseys considered Elvis' appearance to be risky for the program, so it was decided that Elvis' gyrations would not be permitted, and the star was shown only from the waist up. But he was still the show's main attraction.

Milton Berle got Elvis next. He was signed for two guest spots which showed the singer in all his glory. The appearance earned Elvis five thousand dollars.

Berle and Debra Paget, a young actress, joined Elvis in his humping and bumping and brought the house down. If it occurred to Milton Berle that he was doing something daring in presenting Elvis

Presley as the young man actually worked, it was a different Berle than Show Business knew. He had been around long enough to recognize the artistry of an exotic dancer as well as that of a ballerina. He respected young Presley's originality.

A new singer who swung his hips wasn't exactly a novelty in Uncle Miltie's life. A guy named Jolson had been around for a good many years, swatting his backside, shaking his pelvis, and shimmying just as obviously as Elvis Presley. There was a big difference. Jolson, for all his fancy footwork and pelvic manipulations, was far from a sex symbol.

For his professionalism Uncle Miltie was paid off in an avalanche of protests. But the ratings once again showed the impact of Elvis' name on the public. Disregarding the crank mail and telephone calls, NBC held its option on Elvis and next put him on *The Steve Allen Show* which was shown opposite Ed Sullivan's, then at the peak of its power.

When Elvis appeared, he was wearing a tux and tails instead of his usual hot pink and yellow. He was also asked to remain stationary during the entire performance. He was obliged to appear in a sketch with Imogene Coca and Andy Griffith. Elvis managed to look handsome in a Western costume, but that was about the size of it. Some girls were dragged into the proceedings to shriek and faint at the sight of Elvis, giving the Presley camp more ammunition that their idol was being destroyed.

The Allen show afforded Presley fans an opportunity to demonstrate their own outrage. They deluged the network with calls, protesting that toning Elvis down was an insult to an artist and to his audience.

One critic observed, "Mr. Presley appeared a frightened animal caught in the iron bars of a cage. He deserves more respectful treatment than this from his television sponsors who aren't exactly losing audiences with his appearances, controversial though they may be, among the usual well-organized groups dedicated to the art of protesting anything that strays from their narrow conventions."

Elvis Presley's initial TV appearances wrote a bizarre note in the annals of TV ratings. Whatever the program and in spite of the pressure the results remained constant. As ratings soared, the switchboard was swamped with calls. Presley was becoming an object of contention rather than meeting acceptance as an entertainer.

It was a difficult position to sustain, but thanks to Colonel Parker and Elvis, who shared some down-south common sense, they rode out the storm and the Colonel put on his wide-brimmed hat and went over to CBS to sit down and talk to Ed Sullivan about "his boy."

*   *   *

Sullivan was in the position of theatrical impressarios since time began, negotiating from the premise of "Never hire that man again—until we need him."

Sullivan swallowed hard but met the Colonel's

price, fifty thousand dollars for three appearances. The announcement that Sullivan had accepted Elvis for his "family show" produced another avalanche of letters and protests. Sullivan issued the absurd assurance that Elvis would be photographed only from the hips up.

Evidently Elvis had learned a great deal in a short time and had no intention of being thrown to the lions on the biggest opportunity of them all—the *Ed Sullivan Show*. If he couldn't do his own "thing" Elvis intended trying. He'd studied the camera and had devised a way to at least suggest the *total* Elvis. It worked, and of all those controversial early TV appearances, the Sullivan shows came off the best.

Writing in *The Illustrated Elvis*, W.A. Harrison explained how far Elvis had come in a few short weeks:

"On the *Ed Sullivan Show*, where he's told to stay subdued, he manages to be better; he insinuates. Against a dark, light-flecked background, his hair shining with lacquer, he runs through *Don't Be Cruel*, starts to sway just a little—and is promptly cut off at the waist. He then introduces *Love Me Tender*—the title song of his first movie—and he sings it by plunging his fists in his pockets and rocking back and forth. Lazy, greasy and he's Rudolph Valentino—sliding a hand down one thigh, shrugging his shoulders just for kicks, and very slyly mocking the sentiments of the song, sometimes rolling his eyeballs.

"The girls go bananas, their shrieks shake the camera, and Mr. Sullivan is losing pounds as he stands in the wings. Later, Elvis Presley saunters back before the cameras to publicize his newest LP. His hands hang loose and limp, he sways dreamily from side to side, he cups one hand over an ear in an imitation of Johnny Ray, and on the last line of *Love Me*—a long drawn-out 'OOOHH'—he suddenly grabs hold of his head, shakes it vigorously and howls, 'Love me!' as if he's been knifed by a madman. It brings the house down."

A toned-down but subtly insinuating Elvis gave Sullivan a rating of 82.6, an all-time high for the series. The two succeeding telecasts received equally impressive ratings and Ed Sullivan beamed. For all his pious posturing and highly publicized determination to keep his show suitable for the "American family," Sullivan knew top ratings counted. His long years on Broadway told him that often sex appeal separated the superstar from the performer.

What annoys the reporter looking back on the scene in the fifties is the gross hypocrisy of the television networks. Obviously, Elvis' gyrations and style were what the public wanted to see. To compromise a performer because of pressure groups seems as irresponsible as putting something on the airways that was really downright dirty.

Moreover, the network people had been in business long enough to recognize the protestors as middle-Americans who make a hobby of provoking trouble. They are a curious, if well-meaning lot of vocal, cranky individuals, who thrive on contention. They are well organized and their letters, generally couched in identical language, are spun out from mailing lists, often containing non-existent addresses, the names of deceased persons, even names made up out of thin air.

Regardless of protests, sincerely motivated or crank-inspired, Elvis was here to stay. Anyone who dismissed him as a passing fad was making a serious mistake.

Even before Elvis finished his round of TV engagements in New York, it was impossible for him to be seen in public without being mobbed. It began with his arrival for the Sullivan show when he was forced to sneak into town, heading immediately to the Warwick Hotel at 54th Street and Sixth Avenue. He had arrived by train while his group, consisting of three musicians and a quartet called *The Jordanaires*, had driven up from Tennessee.

Within hours, fans had stationed themselves around the Warwick, refusing to move until Elvis came down to talk to them. When a reporter asked about Elvis' immediate plans, Colonel Parker gave a prophetic answer, "Elvis has no plans. Any place he goes, he'll be mobbed, so he won't go any place."

Chapter 5

For many years one of the more perceptive members of the Hollywood press corps has been May Mann, who came to Hollywood in its golden years, a beautiful, statuesque, young woman, barely out of her teens. Today she is still a handsome woman, still writing for newspapers in her native Utah, syndicated widely, besides handling dozens of magazine chores every year.

A few years ago she wrote a fascinating biography of Jayne Mansfield, born of a close association with the star. They regarded themselves as sisters. This has been the key to May's success—her capacity for inviting the confidence and friendship of the stars. May has become more than a newspaperwoman; rather, a personality to whom stars have gone to for help and advice.

May maintained a warm and enduring friendship with Elvis Presley, whom she met early in his film career. Elvis took to her immediately and from that point on, May Mann enjoyed free access to Elvis at all times. The following excerpts are from her biography of Presley called: *The Private Elvis*.

"Elvis was signed for Las Vegas by Sammy Lewis, the enterprising producer at the New Frontier Hotel. This was Elvis' first appearance in a plush Vegas nightclub, and his only one until 1969. Lewis signed Elvis for two weeks at $7,500.00 weekly. Sheckey Greene was second on the bill. A sign of Elvis' figure, fifty-feet high, was put out in front in blazing lights. But Danny Thomas and other well-known entertainers easily outdrew Elvis, the newcomer, who was not then quite ripe for Las Vegas' sophisticated older audiences.

"Elvis spent his time between shows in the local movie house seeing western films. He would see the same western bill over and over again, recalls Mr. Lewis. Elvis also had a penchant for the peanut butter and banana sandwiches that he would have sent up by the dozen to his room. It was also noted that Elvis neither smoked nor drank hard liquor but was fond of cold milk and ice cream sodas. Mr. Lewis, discovering that Elvis was to start his first film in Hollywood, offered Elvis a third week. The Colonel said no. Others said Sheckey Greene was the bigger attraction, but footage of Elvis on stage with a bevy of dancing girls behind him was filmed by The Colonel for a future movie. The Vegas chorus girls dug Elvis and coteried around him on sight.

"To keep him from too much mauling, a group of hometown Memphis boys traveled with him. They were always on hand. When Elvis came through the hotel gambling casinos, and by chance was unnoticed, the boys, prodded by The Colonel, would stand off to the side and start yelling, 'There goes

Elvis Presley!' This created a commotion which Elvis smilingly accepted as part of his job, and he'd sign autographs.

"Timing is everything. Unfortunately it was not until two weeks after his Las Vegas engagement that his new hit records resulted in his picture and story in a big national magazine. People began to realize who *Elvis the Pelvis* was and became more fully aware of his impact.

"His effect on teenage girls grew alarmingly out of hand. Soon vicars and ministers and PTA groups began to voice disgust and great alarm at Elvis' gyrating actions on stage. They denounced him as vulgar! Girls went into hysteria or shock or both on sight of Elvis—they swooned listening to his records. The gyrations of the 'King of Swoon' had the teenagers glassy-eyed with ecstasy. While parents were protesting Elvis' show as lewd, the teenage girls were saying, 'Elvis' voice makes me shiver down to my toes.' Or, 'I feel suddenly nice and warm inside, when I play Elvis' records.'

"'Elvis Presley is sexually setting young American womanhood on fire!' declared ministers. They rose in their pulpits all over America demanding that Elvis be banned. Elvis was accused of actually corrupting thousands of young girls by exciting them physically and emotionally in the wrong way.

"Fan clubs for Elvis at the same time were organized throughout the country with membership cards. The instructions to Elvis Fan Club members read: 'To be members in good standing each week you must send out five postcards to a disc jockey in your vicinity, and follow it up with ten phone calls a week to the radio stations, demanding Elvis' records.' Girls formed Elvis Presley clubs of their own which met at their various homes for Elvis-record sessions. They would scream and cry at every record with over-wrought emotions.

"Boys at first began to tease the girls who were avid Elvis fans. Soon young men were trying to imitate Elvis by singing and wiggling, while department stores stocked cheap guitars and bell-bottom pants, that proved fast sellers. Young men began wearing Presley-like long sideburns.

"Schoolteachers told their classes that Elvis Presley was hurting the teenage generation, with his erotic behavior in public. His sexy gyrations were said to be disgraceful. He was introducing to this young generation a new uninhibited sexual freedom which was declared unhealthy and demoralizing. Boys with long hair and sideburns were always the ones, it was declared, who started trouble in the cafeterias and the classrooms.

"Elvis' imitators were decried as 'awful hood-lums!' Some of the boys were accused of setting their long hair in fingerwaves like Elvis. Elvis was reported going to beauty shops to get his pompa-dour set.

"In Los Angeles, when Elvis appeared for two nights at the Pan Pacific Auditorium, thousands of girls were turned away. The place was packed solid and tickets sold at three-to-five dollars with a dollar for the program. A large contingent of boys imitating Elvis' dress style was on hand.

"At the start, a rock 'n' roll band preceded Elvis. When the star, Elvis himself, walked on stage, everyone began to shout, stamp, jump, scream, and shriek. Extra police were called in to stop the bedlam. They had to stand by helplessly! Who can shut up three thousand screaming teenagers!

"Elvis began to play his guitar. Whatever he had said into the microphone couldn't be heard over the cheers and screaming ovation being accorded to the idol. Elvis strummed his guitar and talked and no one could hear that either. You could see Elvis was singing, but no one could hear a word.

"Elvis finally grabbed one of the mikes, holding it, and he began petting it as though it were a girl or a teddy bear. The latter had now become, he said, his passion. He had long won teddy bears by pitching balls into holders at the fairs! Now he collected teddy bears and never traveled anywhere, even in a car or on a plane, without his big teddy bear for a companion. This of course was The Colonel's idea. Whether Elvis, who was actually on the shy side, was embarrassed or not, he never faltered in carrying out The Colonel's programming.

"With the mike in hand, Elvis began his shimmy wiggles. His whole body was moving from head-to-toe in a sexy frenzy.

"At times he pulled at his clothes as though he wanted to be free of them. Some of the girls fell on the floor as if they were having a fit. Some girls kicked and lashed out their arms. Some grabbed their faces and dug their nails into the flesh. Some closed their eyes and pulled their hair out by the roots. Everyone reacted, caught up in a wild maddening love-in.

"Colonel Parker's shape was seen behind the curtain pushing out a statue of a big dog—the RCA Victor record dog. Elvis who was singing *'Hound Dog,'* began to sing to the dog. He gyrated to the floor and appeared to be making love to the dog as if it were a girl. Elvis moved toward the dog and he rolled over and over. He pushed the dog, and it almost fell off the stage but Colonel Parker pushed it back at Elvis. The fervor of his fans reached fever pitch.

"Elvis kept singing and rolling on the floor. Everyone seemed to go mad. A fourteen-year-old girl began snarling and biting her own arm. Others were rolling in the aisles in convulsions.

"Finally Elvis went off stage, and hundreds of girls rushed up, stomping the security guards. Using their handkerchiefs, they rubbed the floor where Elvis had stood. One grabbed the mike and made love to it. Some girls and some fellows rolled on the floor like they had seen Elvis do. Policemen had to drag them off by force as they screamed and cried incoherently.

"The next morning's newspaper banner headlined, *'Elvis performance disgraceful, lewd and disgusting.'* The police and the vice squad came the second night to make arrests. Elvis, however, had toned down his act. Everyone who'd seen the previous night's show, kept saying, 'But you should have seen Elvis last night.'

"Teenage fans throughout the country made an

uproar. They began to fear for their idol Elvis. They didn't want him to be banned or to lose him. 'Please don't take Elvis from us,' they'd write in thousands of letters to newspapers and to the ministers who were crusading against him.

"Among those aghast at the Presley performance and one of the most vociferous anti-Presley columnists was Hedda Hopper. She spent many columns trying to kill Elvis and The Colonel, decrying them as 'the most obscene vulgar influence on young America today.'

"Years later Miss Hopper had the good sense, she said, to realize that the Twist which she was trying to master one night at a Hollywood nightclub, was actually the gyration that would never have been accepted as a part of Americana if Elvis Presley had not prepared us for it.

"Elvis, brought up as a strict church-going, God-fearing young man, had many qualms obeying The Colonel's showy sensation-seeking tactics in setting him up as a world-wide sex symbol. Gladys and Vernon Presley, reading in their hometown paper that their son was 'demoralizing the youth of America,' that he was *Sir Swivel Hips,* 'a vulgar unworthy idol of the young,' were appalled.

"Elvis consoled them and explained it was all a show to get him known. They must not worry. Trust the Colonel, who knew what he was doing. 'I trust The Colonel,' Elvis said. That was good enough, or had to be, for Gladys and Vernon. 'The Colonel is really like a daddy to me when I'm away from home,' Elvis said. 'He has to make me controversial to get me going. We haven't done anything bad.' The blue noses thought otherwise.

"The Colonel, a good judge at appraising character, had known that Elvis had something else as basic as his obvious sex appeal that drew young women to him like a magnet. He had a quality inside of him that made girls and women alike know that he was a good person; that all of this razz-ma-tazz was a sensational springboard to get him on the glory road to fame.

"Actually by instinct, no matter what he did, how he acted, you knew what he was—that basically Elvis had integrity, honor and good character. You knew that no matter what he was called to do on stage, that he was a nice religious person beyond reproach, who would never change. That made him worthy of being an idealistic idol to believe in and praise, which was accepted and acknowledged by his fans.

"The Colonel had in mind a combination Valentino-Gable in Elvis. He had to start the ball rolling big, and sex is the best ready-seller in any market. While Elvis was being voted the promising country western artist of his time, ironically the press everywhere was blasting him with personal criticism. *'Unfit Hero for Youth,'* said even the Communist press, which took pot shots at Presley when young West German teenagers formed Presley fan clubs. The East German teenagers formed a Presley Ban. *The Young World*, a Communist newspaper, declared the singer was a *'weapon in the American psychological war. His secret function is to recruit youth with unclear political views.'*

"*The Evening Independent* in St. Petersburg, Florida, in the summer of 1956, editorialized on its front pages that Elvis was the Pied Piper of rock 'n' roll, 'a swivel hipped, leg-lashing entertainment bomb who blasted the downtown area into chaos all day yesterday. Screaming fainting teenagers lined the streets early to catch a glimpse of Elvis, a rock billy gyrating singer whose sexy sultry style has caused a revolution!' Some proclaimed, 'We must protect our daughters from the Elvis Presley exposure.'

"'I live with my conscience,' Elvis declared. 'That's what's important. That and my faith in God. It hasn't been all easy,' he admitted. 'But I keep my faith in God, and I want to keep on, so my Mama and my Daddy and my folks will never be poor or hungry again. No one knows how poor and hungry we've been, and how it is when you're sick and there's no money to get a doctor or to get some medicine from the drug store. Or to get even bare necessities without taking food out of your mouth to do it—because there's not enough money for both! My Mama has worked so hard, I want to make it all up to her in every way I can.'

"Elvis and The Colonel cooled the sexy dynamics of his act. The following year Elvis, who was winner of all honors of the teenagers' popularity polls, now discovered when the count came in, he had dropped to fourth place. The press headlined, *Perry Como, the baritone barber of Cannonsburg, Pennsylvania, shaved the sideburns off Elvis Presley to win a flock of honors in the Annual poll.* Elvis' appeal to the bobbysoxers' poll, however, beat out Sinatra from third place in the voting.

"This gave Elvis a lot to think about. Would his popularity hold or vanish? He knew he had a service hitch in the army coming up in his immediate future. Would it all end then?

"Happily at this time Elvis could lay away his gold lamé suits and teddy bears—Hal Wallis, one of motion pictures' most respected and artistic producers, was sitting at home watching television. When he saw Elvis on the Jackie Gleason show, the celebrated starmaker immediately called Elvis for screen tests."

Chapter 6

Over the years Hollywood had seen the big names from other fields come to town with trumpets blaring, only to sneak away a few months later, grabbing the Chief at the downtown Los Angeles station instead of picking up the crack train at Pasadena. That way they escaped the watchful eyes of newsmen.

Hollywood had reason to be cynical about newcomers who either arrived scared to death or convinced that supernatural forces had summoned them to rescue the film colony from disaster. Wise old hands knew that not every talent, however remarkable, transfers easily to the screen. The camera's eye is more critical than audiences, more perceptive than talent scouts, wiser than producers and directors.

The news that Elvis Presley was going to try his hand at filmaking produced yawns from some, doubts by others, optimism by many who'd watched the young man triumph over incredibly difficult situations. If anything, they believed, the camera could only enhance Elvis' smouldering sexuality, pick up the gleam of his roving eyes and make the snarling lip as devastating to female audiences as did Rudolph Valentino's drooped eyelid, Robert Taylor's dimples and Clark Gable's wicked grin.

The air age changed old travel habits. Stars spun around the globe so quickly in the fifties that the press stopped trying to keep up with their arrivals. They waited until they settled in and went about getting interviews the usual way—through filing a request with the studio involved.

Although Hal Wallis was astute and conscientious about his responsibilities, he decided not to launch Elvis personally, although he had been responsible for making film stars of Dean Martin and Jerry Lewis. Wallis' experiences with that celebrated team had left a bitter memory in a career notable for its longevity and Wallis' easygoing, careful style of movie making. There was seldom any temperament involved in a Wallis production— beyond normal differences that sprang up between stars and directors.

Wallis, however, shipped Elvis to 20th Century-Fox for his first picture, a Civil War drama, originally titled *The Reno Brothers,* which eventually became *Love Me Tender*, one of the several songs Elvis sang in the picture.

The elegant Westwood studio, home lot of such great names as Tyrone Power, Betty Grable, Alice Faye, Don Ameche and Henry Fonda among many others, believed its personnel had long since grown accustomed to bumping into celebrities as a matter of course. They were vastly surprised when Elvis turned out something different in the way of headliners. Elvis Presley had transcended superstardom. He was an event.

Elvis arrived in Hollywood with the Colonel, his entourage of male friends from Memphis and his parents. They took the entire eleventh floor of the Knickerbocker Hotel in the center of Hollywood, a good choice at the time, especially for Elvis, a "night person."

When he reported to the studio, expecting his peers would take him for granted or, more likely, ignore him, Elvis—and the film company brass— were astonished by the stir he created. Hundreds of grips, carpenters, extras, studio secretaries, wardrobe people and visitors stopped whatever they were doing to catch a glimpse of Elvis.

They hadn't the faintest idea of what to expect. As Will Rogers said, "All they knew was what they'd read in the newspapers." That had ranged from titillating to nasty. Whatever, they had reason to expect a flashy, exotic sex symbol.

In this respect, Elvis was no disappointment. His clothes, his white Cadillac, his teddy bear—all the trimmings were present. Along with the Colonel and the entourage.

What surprised everyone was Elvis' quietness and politeness. No one could ever recall a star who called people "Sir" and "Ma'am"—except when the line of a film called for it.

When he entered the studio commissary, important stars got up to get a better look at him. All his co-workers spoke highly of the well-mannered young man who never got on a first name basis even with those he met daily.

"That boy," declared his co-star, Richard Egan, "could charm the birds right out of the trees. He was so humble and eager, we went out of our way to help him."

Yet when Elvis interrupted the production to fly back to Tupelo for a homecoming day, a state fair celebration, he was critical of Hollywood and the reception he'd met there. He said that he had been slighted, that people made fun of him and everyone was trying to take advantage of him.

In light of the respect Hollywood's temperamental and catty population gradually felt for Elvis as he quietly plodded through several years of steady movie making, he was perhaps reacting from inexperience and sensitivity, reflecting the small towner's traditional suspicion of big city sophistication.

Still, Elvis never did feel comfortable in the movie capital but even in this respect he wasn't unique. Yet the press thought it was a big deal. In the days of long-term contracts stars made their homes in Hollywood because it was convenient. Modern actors, no longer obliged to be on call at a moment's notice, live where they choose, traveling to Hollywood only when they have an assignment there.

More than a few sigh for the good old days and would settle in the film city in exchange for a good, old-fashioned long-term contract. Too many of today's young stars are here one day and gone the next. Years pass before they find roles worthy of them. They begin to wonder if yesterday's stars were not wise in accepting regular exposure as career insurance.

Just as surprised as the people at 20th Century was the press when Colonel Parker decided his "boy" was ready to talk. They found a serious young man who hadn't been carried away by his success, who tried honestly to answer their questions as directly as he could.

This disarmed the canny old newspaper reporters. Most of their pieces centered around their impressions of the star—their astonishment that he was so pleasant and unspoiled considering the shock waves his early performances precipitated. Having expected to encounter a hoodlum, meeting a young gentleman came as a surprise.

Elvis had done a lot of growing up since coming to Hollywood. He wasn't a kid eager to help his parents out but a star with responsibilities to his family, Colonel Parker, his producer, the public and himself. The Presleys returned to Graceland in Memphis, the beautiful new mansion Elvis acquired for them.

From being around celebrities Elvis discovered the price tag attached to fame. Elvis was aware that Frank Sinatra had once received the same sort of adulation. And long before him, Valentino. Sinatra had been slugged so hard by bad luck and his own mercurial disposition that he was obliged to stage his own comeback, accepting a minor role in *From Here to Eternity* at a fee the equal of a week's stage work in order to qualify in the superstar game. Elvis decided that he might be enduring. He shaved his sideburns. He began dressing more discreetly and he appeared to be less sensational.

"I don't like to be called *Elvis the Pelvis*. It's a childish expression. But if they wanted to call me that, there was nothing I could do about it. I just had to accept it. You accept the good with the bad, the bad with the good," he told one reporter.

Newsmen appreciated his candor. "I'm not kidding myself. My voice alone is just an ordinary voice. What people come to see is how I use it. If I stand still while I'm singing, I'm dead, man! I might as well go back to drivin' a truck."

When a pretty young newspaperwoman, on practically her first assignment in Hollywood, asked Elvis what he felt about the opinion of psychiatrists who said that he represented a sex symbol to kids, Elvis said quietly, "They all think I'm a sex maniac. They're just frustrated old types anyhow. I'm just natural."

Elvis was a refreshing original in his press relations.

* * *

Much was made of Elvis' extravagance, early in his career and later when he was a millionaire, and could afford sending Cadillacs to policemen he barely knew. But there was nothing original about this flashiness he brought to his personal life. Elvis was behaving according to form—exactly as most country and western singers had been doing for years once they hit the jackpot.

They doted on showy things. Success meant more than fame, being recognized on the street or complaining about paying higher taxes than their neighbors. They enjoyed visible signs of wealth—huge homes, sapphire rings, diamonds, fleets of Cadillacs. These made their work worthwhile.

They didn't fuss about capital gains, investing in oil wells that proved duds. They knew enough about the land's habits to be suspicious of anything they couldn't feel or smell within a day's travel of their homes. Buying a pig in a poke was their attitude toward the stock market. In the way he reacted to his fame and wealth, Elvis was no more than a conformist.

He told reporters, "You know, when I was a kid, I'd sit on the porch and watch those long, low cars whiz by. I told myself one of these days I'm gonna have two Cadillacs sittin' out in front of our place, one for my folks and one for me."

Elvis showed no embarrassment in recalling the poverty and privations of his family. His success was his answer to their faith. He often told of the time his father, with tears in his eyes, explained what was happening to his health, that his back was gradually giving way under the strain of hard work, and the day was not far off when he'd just have to cave in.

"As I stood there," Elvis said, "it was as though something snapped inside of me. I was no longer a boy. I was a man, watching another man suffer. That made me grow up. I believe it changed my whole life."

*   *   *

When *Love Me Tender* was completed and ready to open, the studio assumed it had either a smash hit on its hands or a flop. The toss of the coin could go either way. No one had ever devised the perfect formula for transforming a theatrical attraction into a movie star. Remember what happened to Robert Goulet?

The practical time-tested course lay in a massive pre-opening advertising campaign to announce what the trade calls "saturation bookings." This involved printing many times the number of prints usually ordered on a picture, showing the film in literally hundreds of theatres across the country at the same time—day and date bookings.

By the end of the first day you have a good idea of how a picture will go .You wait for the second day to be sure—even if the *King Kong* remake wasn't yet in the record books to prove that unfavorable word-of-mouth advertising can destroy the best ambitions of man and man-made beasts.

Love Me Tender won no kudos from the press. It wasn't expected to, but financially the picture far exceeded 20th Century's expectations. At the end of the week they were doubling the already hyped print order to meet the demand. It was a landslide. Presley was boxoffice and May Mann recalls that it was then she decided to dub Presley *The King*—the logical successor to Clark Gable's title. Elvis was the new *Golden Boy* of Hollywood.

Love Me Tender had a Grade B look about it

which was unfortunate, but Elvis was far from inept in a sincere portrayal of an innocent ploughboy who falls in love with, and then marries his brother's girl friend. The brother, thought to have been killed by the Yankees during the Civil War, returns to start life over again, a situation that creates inevitable and predictable complications.

From the return of the brother, *Love Me Tender* worked itself into a confused series of episodes involving gunfire. In one of these gunfire duels, Clint Reno (the Presley character) is killed, affording the star an opportunity to perform in a ghostly finale, singing after he's passed on.

The plot didn't matter. Presley did. So did his songs. Working against sharp professionals like Debra Paget, Richard Egan and Mildred Dunnock, Presley more than held his own, emerging very much the star, a believable, sincere personality.

Elvis had come full circle. The kids who discovered him were right all along. He'd burst forth like warm sunshine. And now, as they had on television, in concert, and records, they could joyfully wrap him and his new music up as their own. They had found a hero they could relate to. His songs were extensions of themselves.

Love Me Tender was only the beginning of Elvis' movie career. It proved what Elvis wanted to believe about himself—that he wasn't a flash in the pan, a temporary visitor to the entertainment scene, but someone with particular talent who earned his credentials as a star. He intended to stay around and often said, "I hope that people remember me."

No one thought then that it was more than a statement reflecting ambition, the desire of any artist to leave behind a catalogue of work that would prove durable. It was the kind of statement professionals attach little significance to, being an aspiration a performer might consider at twenty-six or sixty-six.

*   *   *

While Elvis was making *Love Me Tender*, reporters, scrounging for every available tidbit about Presley, obtained information from Elvis' draft board in Memphis that he had been sent a questionnaire to bring his status up to date. His status at the time was 1-A, but since there were several hundred ahead of him in that category, it was fairly early to predict a time when Elvis might be called for service.

A month or so later one of the entertainment industry's trade papers published a totally inaccurate story saying that Presley, when drafted, would be assigned to duty in *Special Services*, the *Entertainment Branch* of the Army, operating out of Fort Dix in New Jersey. Moreover, he would not have to endure the traditional G.I. haircut and furloughs would enable him to continue his film career and keep his recording and television dates.

The story was totally inaccurate and irresponsible although, in theory, it was not improbable. During World War II, the Armed Services had a variety of deals going with prominent personalities, enabling them to keep their professions going and still perform military duties. In many cases, especially those involving over-age stars who volunteered, the special privileges proved valuable to the war effort.

But in no way would Elvis Presley be able to enjoy the same consideration, not even if it came as the result of a presidential proclomation.

Typical of the impact of the story, however, and the fantastic potency of the Presley name, was shown by the fact that the story had barely gotten off the presses before a Chicago radio station recorded a song *Leave My Sideburns To Me*. This was just one of many songs, using Elvis as a theme. They ranged from *Hey, Mr. Presley* and *Dear Elvis* to *Elvis Presley for President*.

An arranger concocted the *Elvis Presley Blues* and for Christmas Mary Kaye told about a little girl who promised to clean her teeth and eat her Wheaties if she found Elvis under her Christmas tree in lyrics that read, *I don't want a bracelet or diamonds. I just want Elvis instead.*

Around this time another young singer, Pat Boone, began to make an impact, and the contrast of the two personalities offered a festival of irony. Pat was the clean-cut, all-American boy, whittled to perfection. He'd gotten a college degree. He sang religious songs but in straight rhythm—unlike Elvis who added his special beat. Boone was the singer in the "grey flannel suit"—the short-haired gentleman in a blue blazer. He was married and a father, while Elvis was credited with quips like, "Why buy a cow when you can get milk under the fence?"

With his singles, first two albums and his second picture, *Loving You*, all smashing box office records, Elvis was in virtually an unassailable position as the most extraordinary entertainer of all time. There had never been anyone like him before—a top star commanding big money in all the media constantly outgrossing himself. The only artist Elvis competed against in this Golden Era of his career was *himself*.

Hal Wallis personally took charge of *Loving You*. In production values, it emerged a far superior effort to Elvis' first flick. It was the first of Elvis' films that tried to be autobiographical. Elvis portrayed a young truck driver, discovered by a press agent, Lizabeth Scott. He goes from small-time appearances to the S.R.O. category, very much as Elvis did.

The fans liked it because despite the plot's obviousness and the gimmicks employed to introduce songs, *Loving You* offered a character closer to the real Elvis. It gave the illusion of a behind-the-scenes look into his professional and private life.

Until Hollywood, Elvis had been on the move so much that little was known about his love affairs except what reporters gleaned from talking to the young people who'd been at school during his years at Humes. Gladys Presley was the source for the fairly circumspect details of his first crush—the pretty young thing he watched from afar until he summoned the courage to date her.

In Hollywood, Elvis lived in a goldfish bowl and although he could move around the haunts of the film people with less fear of being mobbed, he lived under constant scrutiny by the town's international press corps. In the pre-war years it numbered more than three hundred reporters. By the fifties, their ranks had thinned considerably as Hollywood diminished as an exciting news beat.

Those who'd weathered the rollbacks were the top pros, men and women who knew the Hollywood scene backwards and could project with uncanny foresights the personalities the public might be most interested in. They didn't have to read the polls to know Presley was their hottest circulation builder. Elvis automatically ranked as the top candidate for the kind of headlines fan magazines specialized in: *Elvis' Secret Girl, Number One In Elvis' Little Black Book*, or *Guess Who's Ecstatic Over Elvis?*

But they didn't have to reach into the Central Casting Directory for obscure, pretty girls to serve as mystery playmates in Elvis' private life. There were plenty of live wires on his list.

Debra Paget, his leading lady in *Love Me Tender* was his first official date and word went out that the pretty dark-haired starlet was crazy about him. Debra was given some great lines by the publicity department. "The *electric ecstasy* Elvis stimulates in women is almost unbelievable! I learned this when we made *Love Me Tender*. What is that *something* Elvis has? I'm not sure I can explain it."

Louis Armstrong once said the same thing about jazz; "If it's gotta be explained to you, you don't understand it."

Time cleared up a lot of misinformation spread about. Evidently things were not really that warm between Debra and Elvis. They got along on the set and, like many young co-stars, sometimes dated. Debra, it turned out, had another man in her life, Howard Hughes. The press found a way to conveniently terminate what had probably not been a serious romance to begin with.

Natalie Wood was next in Elvis' list of conquests. She was a lively, vivacious girl, brought up in Hollywood, who knew the score and possessed a sense of humor about the place that a newcomer like Elvis needed badly.

Natalie was as comfortable at the film town's posh dining places as at the hamburger joints that seemed to suit Elvis better. She may have been horrified watching him wolf down hamburger after hamburger, washed down with malted milks. But Natalie wasn't picky. Elvis was a big boy who burnt up a lot of energy in the course of a day.

To please him Natalie took up Elvis' hobby of motorcycling. They went to Memphis together and were spotted there by the press, "a duo on a motorcycle," riding around the countryside. Immediately a love affair was written into it. It made great photos and good copy.

It also made both young people uncomfortable. Natalie, more used to them, accepted the photographers and the paragraphs in the columns with the grace born of years of experience. Presley caught the full impact of being a giant-sized celebrity. There was literally no place he could go without drawing a crowd. Someone would telephone the newspapers who'd send out photographers—and it was the old cat and mouse game.

Elvis hadn't reached the stage of some headliners who preferred slugging photographers to cooperating. He realized publicity and Colonel Parker's flamboyant promotion had made him a star. Elvis wasn't about to bite the hand that fed him. Gradually it became more comfortable to retreat from the public scene, isolating himself, beginning what in retrospect were the greatest years of his life—as well as the loneliest.

Neal Matthews, one of the *Jordanaires* said, "The only time he could get out was at night. He'd rent a skating rink and skate all night and whoever was around would drop over to see him." Sometimes Elvis rented an entire movie house inviting only close friends to come along. Like any normal young man, he was reluctant to be alone.

He didn't realize that he was reducing his human contacts by steadily pulling away from the crowd. It was an unhealthy situation. So was the alternative. Going out meant more than risking losing the buttons off his clothes; there existed a danger stars were well aware of—losing a limb or getting konked in the head.

Natalie eventually saw less of Elvis. The rock star, who'd never been previously exposed to the experienced public personality, expressed regret in his individualistic way, saying that professional women put their ambitions above anything else. He saw them as competitive women who, without this characteristic, couldn't have gotten where they were.

"The trouble is," Elvis said, "they carry the drive

to be tops into their homes and they tend to forget the pride of the man in the house."

* * *

In the absence of any hot news about Elvis, the press whipped out a paragraph or two about his draft status. He'd reported for his physical at his Memphis draft board where the military men refused any comment about the star's health or rating in the *Intelligence Tests* that preceded induction or rejection. A spokesman simply said that Presley's draft status remained 1-A.

Then there was speculation as to whether there would be efforts to defer the star to accommodate his contractual commitments. This met angry response from Memphis Draft Board officials who stated that "deferments of the kind suggested were not its policy." Through it all, Elvis remained calm and unperturbed. He knew his home town better than the movie titans and so did the Colonel.

They stockpiled a series of recordings that could be distributed at regular intervals during Elvis' Army duty, fully aware that he faced induction and there would be no "deals." Elvis would take whatever assignment came along without asking for special privileges.

As for placing Elvis in *Special Services* where he'd be on call to entertain thousands of servicemen, their friends and everyone within driving distance of a mainland or overseas post, the thought brought cold sweat to the brow of Colonel Parker! Not his "boy." Singing for all those potential cash customers at the military pay of the era, seventy-eight dollars a month! That would have been highway robbery—stealing the kid's birthright and condemning the Colonel to an old age home for paupers!

King Creole, filmed in 1958, amounted to Elvis' biggest money deal. His guarantee was five hundred thousand dollars and fifty percent of the profits. That was before million dollar salaries became status symbols of the stars. For its time, it was virtually unprecedented.

Elvis himself wrote a letter to his draft board asking for a sixty day deferment from January 20 to March 20 to allow the completion of his picture, pointing out that either its cancellation or shutdown would result in an unhappy Christmas for all those involved so long in the movie's preparation. It was shrewd and tasteful, far more intelligent than the high-handedness shown by studio heads in requesting deferments during World War II. They stepped over local draft boards to make arrangements with Washington big shots.

The deferment was granted, although some publicity grabbers in Memphis' Draft Boards registered dissent with grandiose statements opposing the deferment.

One said, "I cannot conscientiously ask any mountain boy to serve the country unless afforded the same treatment as Mr. Presley." He overlooked the fact that at the depths of World War II, when military manpower was sorely needed, local draft boards were generous and considerate in granting deferments, especially short-term postponements, thirty and sixty days.

On March 24, Elvis reported to his Memphis draft board, accompanied by his parents. Newspaper reporters from all over the world were on hand to witness the induction. They bombarded him with a barrage of absurd questions and Elvis managed polite answers to all of them, summing up his attitude with the statement, "I simply want to be treated like all the other fellows."

Chapter 7

Elvis' military career began with history's most publicized haircut. Presley fans mourned the shaving of Elvis' sideburns and the shearing of his famous pompadour. Colonel Parker sighed characteristically, "I know a lot of people that would pay a lot of money for that hair."

Elvis resorted to an old bromide, "Hair today, gone tomorrow," as he paid the military fee of sixty-five cents for the cut.

Like Delilah's shearing of Samson's locks, Elvis worshippers claimed that after his G.I. haircut Elvis was never the same again. They were right, but more than a haircut produced the real changes Elvis experienced while in service. Elvis was twenty-three and for the very first time in his life he was completely on his own, placed in a difficult position where neither his parents nor Colonel Parker could help him.

Press and fans followed every move Elvis made from his arrival at his Memphis Draft Board to Fort Chaffee, Arkansas. After the bus crossed the Mississippi River and stopped on the other side for a break, fans stormed the cafe, located Elvis trying to grab some food, tore the buttons off his clothes and escaped with Elvis' fountain pen.

After induction proceedings were completed at Fort Chaffee, the Army announced that Elvis would undergo basic training at Fort Hood in Texas with the Second Armored Division. Once inside the military establishment, a wall of privacy was erected between Elvis and the public that almost worked. Public relations officials announced that it was against Army policy for inductees to be interviewed during this critical period of their training. Elvis became "off limits" for a couple of months at least.

Still, it wasn't easy. Elvis had as many fans, curiosity seekers and hecklers inside the Fort as out. But thanks to his sympathetic barracks buddies a bodyguard of sorts was thrown around him. "They treat me like anyone else. They consider themselves for just what they are—GI's—the same as me. That's the way I want it."

Elvis' basic training was completed in time for him to attend the Memphis premiers of *King Creole*, which enjoyed the benefit of a lot of talent besides Elvis'. Hal Wallis was the producer, the story originated as a Harold Robbins novel, with a screenplay by Herbert Baker and Michael Vincent Gazzo. Michael Curtiz was the director.

It is difficult to identify writers' contributions in films when so many different hands are involved in the final screenplay. However, the presence of Herbert Baker as part of the writing team may have accounted for the realistic parts of the characterization written for Elvis.

Herbert Baker was the son of Belle Baker, one of the great singing stars of vaudeville and Broadway revues. Herbert was a footlights kid who knew the backstage better than his own home. As a child he frequently performed with his mother and embracing a writing career in Hollywood came naturally to him. He grew up in the Prohibition Era and had more than a nodding acquaintance with hoods who infiltrated Show Biz—the sort of unsavory characters that peopled *King Creole*.

With Michael Curtiz at the helm of a cast that included, besides Presley, Carolyn Jones, Walter Matthau, Dolores Hart and Dean Jagger, *King Creole* came over as the best of Presley's first musicals.

It told the story of a young boy in New Orleans trying to make it as a singer, who gets involved with mobsters and fights to save himself. The reviews were uniformly favorable and the New York *Times* critic Howard Thompson wrote: "As the lad himself might say, cut off my legs and call me Shorty! Elvis Presley can act."

The *Times* review was icing on the cake of a universally favorable press and Elvis was walking on air. But Elvis' life had been *all-career* for so long, that he'd almost forgotten that there was a personal side that would have to absorb shocks as rough as the snide remarks of TV critics, or the thundering denunciation by pressure groups.

*   *   *

Gladys Presley was a soft, gentle, quiet-spoken woman regarded by Elvis and Vernon with awe because of her enormous vitality. It was no secret that Gladys was the keystone of the family, the optimist who could foresee a brighter tomorrow regardless of the bleakness of today.

Elvis noticed a change in his mother when he returned to Memphis for the *King Creole* festivities. She appeared to have lost some of her energy; the sparkle was missing from her usual bubbly personality.

There was concern but nothing serious. Gladys was only forty-two with a history of good health, a basically strong woman. Taken to the hospital, doctors examined Gladys and her condition was diagnosed as hepatitis.

Only a few weeks later, Elvis was given a sudden emergency leave to fly to his mother's bedside. Gladys Presley had suffered a heart attack. Elvis remained at her bedside for thirty-six hours without sleeping and finally went home because his father insisted. Three hours later his father called. Gladys was dead.

Elvis went into a state of shock that lasted until after the funeral. When he arrived at the hospital, he threw himself across his mother's body, sobbing uncontrollably. He tried to express his feelings to newspapermen, but he found it impossible to talk. For once, they respected the young man's feelings and left him alone.

Elvis erected a huge monument at the Memphis Cemetery to the memory of his mother and whenever he returned to Memphis thereafter he visited the memorial.

Gladys' age varies from account to account. She was at least forty-two, probably forty-three or four. The year or so Gladys Presley may have snipped off her age doesn't alter the fact that she died a very young woman.

Friends, neighbors, those who met her only in the years of Elvis' professional career, were impressed with Gladys Presley. She was a strong, vital woman, greatly pleased by her son's success. But there was the mother's great concern for Elvis—the grinding schedule he'd been on since rising to stardom. She wasn't a stage mother in the usual sense—getting in everyone's hair. That wasn't her style.

She left the details of managing Elvis to the Colonel. Like Vernon and Elvis, she trusted him completely. But she wasn't indifferent to the fact that Elvis was just a kid, thrust into a blinding spotlight for which he was far from prepared. She cringed at every nasty word printed about Elvis, despite his reassurance that it was all part of the "act." Gladys may have been a country woman, but that didn't make her unworldly or unaware.

She fretted over the demands imposed on Elvis, the long hours of rehearsal, travel, the strain of the performances themselves. "He'll be dead before he's thirty," Gladys warned as she followed him through his back breaking, nerve-shattering schedule that began at a recording studio in Memphis and led to stardom in Hollywood. She begged Elvis to slow down.

100

His mother's death, Elvis believed, foreshadowed his own—early and shocking. He always believed that. He frequently talked about death, accepting as a matter of inevitability that he would not live long past his mother's age. He likened himself to Bobby Darin, a close friend, who suffered from heart trouble and died at an early age. Elvis went so far as to predict his own death at forty, missing the actual time by only two years.

There is no way to describe the anguish that Elvis felt for months to come. Gladys was the force that had given Elvis his drive. She was the only permanent woman in his life, and one wonders if that accounted for his disinclination to consider marriage seriously during her lifetime.

On her gravestone Elvis had inscribed, *She Was The Sunshine Of Our Life*, a tribute that could not possibly explain the bond that existed between Gladys and her boy.

* * *

A month after Gladys' death, Elvis was assigned to duty in Germany. Although he'd been a soldier for about six months, public interest in Elvis showed no signs of diminishing despite the prediction of one newspaperman who wrote, "Before Presley learns to salute properly, his public will have forgotten him."

To give his point some emphasis, he recalled that Clark Gable had never really come back, overlooking that Gable was a middle-aged man, accepted by the Army for his value as a morale booster rather than his skill at soldiering.

Elvis Presley was a kid whose career had barely gotten off the ground—even if the controversy he stirred up gave the impression that Presley had been around forever.

At a press conference before he sailed to Germany, he spoke of the loss he felt at his mother's passing, saying that she had been a friend who would let him talk to her at any hour of the day or night if he had a problem.

He told reporters that his family—and the irrepressible Colonel Parker—would be following him to Germany and that as far as he could tell, his fan mail, far from decreasing, was running about fifteen thousand letters a week. "It's driving them crazy at Fort Hood."

Asked what kind of girl Elvis wanted, Presley answered, "Female, sir."

There were plenty of females waiting for him in Germany where his records had quickly been appreciated. Elvis' influence found an eager response among German youth whose problems in the fifties were, in many ways, more tragic than those of their American brothers. They were outcasts in the family of nations. They felt the urgency of rejecting their elders and anything stamped U.S.A. represented their hopes for the future. Elvis was no less their idol than he was America's Pied Piper.

They rejected the *lederhosen* German youth had worn for generations and paid outrageous prices for "genuine" American-made bluejeans. Although short-cropped Prussian hair had disappeared a generation earlier, they quickly adopted Elvis' style of dress as they snapped up his disks and looked for bounce, bumps and grinds in their own singers.

Young German singers couldn't quite grab the Presley style, but they did come up with *ersatz* personalities and new rhythms. A whole crop of youthful entertainers appeared to replace Germany's tired, old stars. The revolution had been as complete and devastating as in the United States, occurring almost overnight.

So when Elvis' troop ship arrived at Bremerhaven there were thousands of screaming German kids waiting to greet him. The Army maneuvered their soldier-star into a troop train and Elvis landed kiss-proof at his permanent station, Friedberg, a village near Frankfurt.

Elvis was assigned a job as a scout-jeep driver, and the information officer who announced Presley's duties made it clear that "it was the kind of job given to soldiers of above normal capability. These men must be able to work on their own, read maps, draw sketches, know tactics and recognize the enemy and enemy weapons."

His family followed soon thereafter, found a house, and when Elvis moved out of the barracks, there was a mild furor that "favoritism" was being shown. It was an empty volley for, under Army regulations, a soldier was permitted to live off-base with his family and dependents. Elvis was strictly within his rights. The new Presley home was situated in Bad-Homberg, a resort spa nearby and he commuted daily to his military duties.

He hadn't been serving abroad very long before he met Priscilla Beaulieu, a young girl of fourteen. Her father was an Air Force captain stationed in Frankfurt which made it difficult for the two young people to meet as often as they would like.

So the newspapers were busy keeping up with the German fraüleins in Elvis' life. American soldiers in Germany were supposed to date the blonde beauties. Why should Elvis be an exception?

According to his superior officers he was performing everything by the book, doing assignments without complaining publicly, griping in private, making a few friends among the GIs and practicing karate. Elvis' hitch, in these respects, was perfectly normal.

Priscilla stuck in Elvis' mind. He had seen her grow up and when it was time for him to leave, now a sergeant, she was a beautiful young lady who drove to the airport and kissed him goodbye. Elvis broke a self-imposed silence about keeping his feelings private, even from his buddies. But with Priscilla it was different. He spoke of her often and affectionately. Priscilla's name slipped into the press occasionally and there had been pictures snapped of Elvis with the girl.

There was no attempt to hide her, but the press seemed not to take the friendship seriously. Once Elvis left Germany she was forgotten. Presley-watchers assumed she was just another girl in his little black blook.

Moreover, Elvis' return was the big news. Colonel Parker was busy with elaborate arrangements for a

Elvis:

THE LONELY STAR

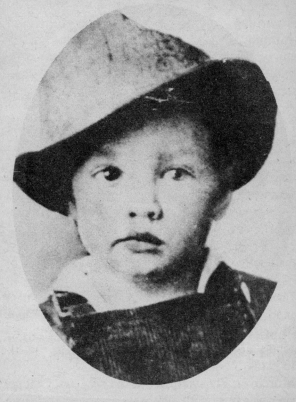

Elvis Presley at age 3, an only child whose twin brother had died at birth.

The house where Elvis was born in Tupelo, Miss., has become a tourist attraction.

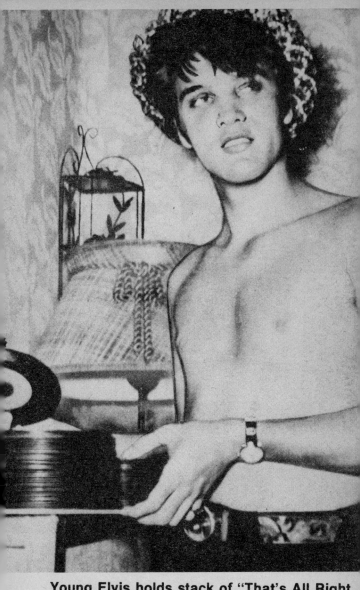

Young Elvis holds stack of "That's All Right, Mama" records that started it all.

Elvis kissed mama Gladys, said goodbye to daddy Vernon and left for Army in 1958.

Elvis mustered out of Army at Fort Dix, N.J.
By now his beloved mom was dead.

By 1960 even established superstars like Frank Sinatra were accepting Elvis.

One of the few reporters to have a close relationship with Elvis was famed May Mann.

El looked like young Brando, but Marlon was difficult—Elvis was easy to work with.

In 1967, Elvis wed Priscilla Beaulieu, and
thought his loneliness had ended.

In 1969, Elvis and Priscilla still looked like
newlyweds—but trouble was brewing.

With dad Vernon in Las Vegas where he'd playing to huge, sellout audiences again.

By 1972, Elvis was hot on
concert trail—which left
lots less time for folks
back home.

After the Presleys divorce, Priscilla was seen often with Mike Stone, karate expert.

Lisa Presley was hurt by her parents' divorce—but remained her daddy's girl.

Hours before death, Elvis set Christmas, 1977, as day he would wed Ginger Alden.

On day after his death, 80,000 gathered outside his home to mourn a lonely man.

Welcome Home, Elvis series of events, engagements and visits that would make the two men richer than they already were. Presley, back in the spotlight, was a far more dynamic personality to write about than Elvis, the eligible bachelor.

Elvis' two years of military service had not whittled away at his popularity. His records, carefully spaced in their distribution, leaped to the top of the charts. Elvis returned home three million dollars richer than when he left.

Hal Wallis, as eager as the Colonel to have his star back, nearly fainted away when the Colonel printed up a phony newspaper page, carrying the banner headline: PRESLEY RE-ENLISTS.

*   *   *

While the razzle-dazzle of his re-entry into Show Biz was being masterminded by the Colonel and impressarios chewed their nails, eager for a crack at the boxoffice gold Elvis produced, the young man must sometimes have wondered where he stood at this stage of his life.

He was twenty-five years old. His triumphs were on the books. The deprecations were there too. But was he the "dirty young man" of the fifties, the sexy "fiend" whose mere presence despoiled America's girlhood?

No, indeed. Elvis had found acceptance in the critical court of public opinion. The dignity of his Army life impressed people. He'd modified the frenzy of his early performances. The flashy clothes, the long hair, sideburns, all the affectations once described as "grotesqueness" had become part of the scene.

What was outlandish in attire, absurd in music, offensive in attitude a decade earlier were now commonplace. Elvis Presley had revolutionized a whole generation's life style. He was the catalyst who had led his generation out of the limbo of the fifties into the aggressive sixties.

At the same time, his own image had altered and been modified. Inevitably his image changed and so would Presley. He had matured. Now it was time to reach out for a larger audience than he'd enjoyed before. Time to take advantage of being a superstar in every sense of that much abused description. He could name his fee and conditions in any part of the world, in whatever medium he chose. It was an extraordinary position for a performer his age to be in. Moreover, it was totally without precedent.

Yet there was a hollowness about it that Elvis felt keenly. It began when he suffered the loss of his mother, a traumatic experience he endured with quiet dignity. Yet Elvis often wondered if somehow his success had not affected her health. "She was only forty-two," he said. "She had lived just long enough to know that all her sacrifices were not in vain." Yet, those years of constant attention to her son, travelling with him—they were unaccustomed pressures Gladys was unprepared for.

"But all I wanted for her was to be alive, alive to share all the good things that were coming, the things she deserved," Elvis said.

Elvis kept asking himself why his mother died just at a time when he was able to give her so much. This was bitter irony for a young man, devoted to his mother. Finding it hard to accept, he looked to his religious background for an answer, wondering if perhaps he had done something bad. Brooding produced no answers. Self-accusation was followed by emptiness—an emptiness that lived on.

Elvis had been nervous about being assigned to another country. Foreign travel was an experience that wasn't part of his dreams when he was a kid in Tupelo, Mississippi. White Cadillacs, yes. Europe and the world beyond, no. But the overseas assignment helped distract him from the immediate tragedy.

Being a good soldier in a peacetime Army should hardly have been a challenge to any young man with Elvis' physical strength and easy going personality. The problem lay in being who he was. If you choose to look at it realistically, Elvis became the victim of horrendous discrimination because he knew the minute he set foot on the troop ship that carried him overseas, he could never be himself. Someone, a stranger, a curiosity seeker, a newspaperman; sometimes, a friend, would always be there—looking over his shoulder—ready to pounce on any false step he made.

None of the pleasures of the average GI were his—taking advantage of weekend passes and furloughs to go out and enjoy himself. To find any human recreation, dating a girl, seeing a movie, watching a sports event, driving in the country, Elvis was forced to make elaborate preparations. Always a shy, quiet, private individual, he took to secrecy and slyness. There was no other way to duck the crowds, avoid the press, evade the unending curiosity about himself.

His insurance against becoming "some sort of nut" was the companionship he found in a select group of buddies, in the love of his family, the dates he managed to make, in watching, as he put it later, Priscilla Beaulieu grow up.

Elvis didn't invent loneliness but he was a victim of it. His return to the bright lights only marked the beginning of the loneliness that would thread its way through the rest of his life, isolating him from a world he gave so much pleasure to.

Almost everyone in the world is lonely one way or another. The easiest way to be lonely is to be alone.

The hardest way—also the most common—is to find loneliness when surrounded by a crowd of people, all of whom are either friends or at the very least, friendly acquaintances.

And that was where Elvis Presley stood as he shed his uniform to re-enter his profession. He knew what he'd left behind was only the curtain raiser on the denials that lay ahead. The price of fame—another overworked Show Biz phrase—had already extracted more penalties from Elvis Presley than any other artist in history.

Sinatra's squealers, manipulated largely by clever press agent gimmickry, an early tactic employed by the Colonel, had worn themselves out after a year or so. There were few spots in the United States where

Elvis Presley could stand for more than five minutes without attracting a crowd.

*   *   *

Frank Sinatra assigned himself the role of host to Elvis' professional return in a television extravaganza which was to be filmed as the last of a series of *specials* Sinatra had contracted to do for *Timex*, the watch company. Sinatra had not fared well on TV and his third show, featuring dancer Juliet Prowse, failed to enhance Sinatra's draw as a TV entertainer. Not that Sinatra ever dropped into the last ten but a star of his magnitude was expected to enjoy a wider constituency than the ratings established.

For both entertainers the teaming was shrewd. Presley's camp could—and did—maintain that Sinatra needed the younger man more than Presley needed Sinatra. "Who needs who" is always a highly debatable question in the entertainment business. Value is determined by expediency. The Colonel was smart. He'd muffled Elvis when he was abroad. There were his pictures to keep the name alive, the new records and the old.

A taste of Presley, doing a spot on a show headlined by the biggest singing star in the business, was the kind of homecoming party Parker liked. The pay was good. His "boy" risked nothing. If the ratings remained the same, they could say the show had drawn only the Sinatra crowd. If they zoomed, as Parker fully believed they would, then the credit would go to Presley. Parker held all the cards and

Sinatra didn't wince when the fee was pronounced, one hundred and twenty-five thousand dollars!

Elvis travelled from Memphis to Miami where he had been recording with the Jordanaires, Scotty Moore and D.J. Fontana, doing his first post-war discs, *Stuck On You* and *Fame and Fortune*. Before the recording session had even started, firm orders were already in for a million platters.

Presley's train trip was like a presidential campaign. People lined the railway and Elvis stood on the rear platform, waving to the crowd. It was a beautifully arranged stunt—whose art lay in the fact that not too much arranging was required.

All Colonel Parker needed was to send word down the line that Elvis would be travelling by train; word-of-mouth took care of the rest.

By this time Presley was a genuine folk hero. All his fans needed was a gentle nudging by the Colonel. The days of surrounding him with an entourage of young men yelling, "Here comes Elvis Presley! Make way for Mr. Presley," belonged to the past.

So did the performers Sinatra assembled to tape the special. They were all old-timers. Dean Martin, Sammy Davis, Jr., Joey Bishop and Peter Lawford had been collected to perform a sketch, *The Summit*, which they'd done in Vegas but had never played on the air. There would be the usual "in" banter among Sinatra and his pals. The rest of the hour featured Sinatra's typical and beautifully performed songalogue. There was a brief solo spot for Elvis and another segment in which the two singers, represent-

126

ing different generations, would reprise each other's top songs.

It couldn't have been a comfortable experience for either performer. As soon as Elvis' fans discovered he was at the Fontainebleau Hotel, they began overrunning the place. As for Elvis, he wasn't exactly at home in the company of the cool old pros who laughed at one another's jokes before they heard the tag lines. Moreover, Elvis realized the show would be taped in front of a largely Sinatra audience, to whom his style, tamed down or not, would appear far out.

There was a remarkable feature of Colonel Parker's management of Elvis Presley. It amounted to his willingness to let his "boy" walk into a lion's cage, absolutely confident of his ability to handle the lions.

Having gotten an extraordinary price for Presley, the Colonel let slide demands another manager might make. He protested the kind of audience, knowing Elvis would be overpowered by Sinatra's claque. But his protests were mild and low-keyed.

The Colonel would have preferred Elvis in one of his more familiar costumes. But like the veterans, Elvis locked himself into a tuxedo. To the uninitiated, it might seem the Colonel was "giving his boy away."

But was it all that simple? Not quite. Colonel Parker wanted no hassle with Sinatra. He couldn't afford to allow Elvis to come out a heavy against a real heavyweight. Why challenge something that would agitate the fans? Elvis in a tux? They'd hate it.

So when Elvis next appeared in television he'd have a built-in audience curious about what his "boy" would be wearing. The Colonel liked keeping people guessing. "Always make them want a lot more of Elvis" was how Parker explained his showmanship.

For all his temperament, Sinatra was a sure-footed professional, a little overcome by Elvis' calling him "Mr. Sinatra." His *special* reflected taste and showmanship, even if it emerged finally on the dull side. Presley sang his current hits, *Stuck On You* and *Fame and Fortune*. He borrowed Sinatra's *Witchcraft* for the wind-up, leading the two into *Love Me Tender*.

Joey Bishop, dressing down the corridor from Elvis, decided that his niece in New Jersey might like an autographed picture. So he sent his man Friday to get one. The man returned and told Bishop, "The Colonel stands guard in front of Elvis' dressing room. You can't go in. So I asked him for an autograph from Elvis. He said that Elvis would be pleased to give an autograph for one dollar. That included a photograph."

Stunned, Bishop asked, "Did you tell the Colonel it was for me?"

"Sure, and the Colonel said, 'In that case it should be ten dollars.'"

The show, titled *Frank Sinatra's Welcome Home Party for Elvis Presley* was aired a few weeks later to ratings of 41.5, knocking out all the competition. Sinatra's money paid off. He scored a big one and if the ratings were due to the presence of Elvis, the snarling reviews the show received were also because of him.

Television critics, smarting under the public's continued refusal to take seriously their haughty analyses of the popular medium, clung to their old targets; Elvis' hitch in the Army had not altered their antagonism. They complained that Elvis seemed uncomfortable, which was probably true. *Billboard* managed to applaud his singing but a phrase-maker on the New York *Times* figured he'd found a good one in: *Although Elvis became a sergeant in the Army, as a singer he never left the awkward squad.*

G.I. Blues was an obvious title for Presley's return to movies. It was his first one-woman love story and contrary to the title, there was nothing blue about it (at least not to Paramount—the film grossed four million plus.)

It was a warm, sentimental story about two people who get their wires crossed, with Juliet Prowse playing opposite Elvis as a cabaret dancer with the not-uncommon name of cabaret dancers, Lil. In settling a bet about making out with Lil, Elvis falls in love with her and, after some complications, they manage to realize that the joke's on them—they really dig each other.

Presley purists deplored the absence of strong rock 'n' roll numbers and they were disappointed in the music generally, complaining that little of it did justice to Elvis' talent. Regardless, the picture was a smash and one song, *Wooden Heart*, became another Presley hit record.

G.I. Blues belongs to early Presley movies which are rated among his best. Many partisans felt that Elvis should have enjoyed greater leeway in deciding which films to accept and which to reject. They believed, probably correctly, that Elvis was basically a good enough actor to have met stronger challenges than were offered in the romantic comedies and action pictures with music with which he was identified.

The life and career of Elvis Presley was riddled with paradoxes. He was, as has been noted repeatedly, an original, an innovator, one-of-a-kind. Yet, in films, he brought only his volcanic personality, tamed down considerably, but still showing flashes of the Presley fans found in his records and on the stage.

The films were strictly formula, seldom touched with imagination that veered in the slightest degree from the old Hollywood formula—*play it safe and pick up profits. Fool around with a personality and all you pick up are the pieces.*

Chapter 8

After Elvis returned from Germany he kept in touch with Priscilla Beaulieu, having found himself unable to get her out of his mind. But his emotions weren't totally centered around Priscilla. There was room in Elvis' life for reunions with old girl friends as well as making the acquaintance of new ones. He resumed an old friendship with a Memphis girl, Barbara Hearn, a soft-spoken beauty who accompanied him on his triumphant visit to his home town, Tupelo, which celebrated the return of its favorite son with a county fair.

Another Memphis girl seen with Elvis before and after his military service was Anita Wood, a singer-actress. He had given her a lovely sapphire and she went with friends to be near him when he was stationed at Fort Hood during basic training. She was at Elvis' side when his mother died and was the girl Elvis kissed "good-bye" when he left for Germany.

When all the time they'd been close to each other was counted, it amounted to six years, and those close to the couple felt sure they were in love and would marry. Anita came to Hollywood when Elvis was making *G.I. Blues*. It was a furtive, unbilled visit, few friends knew she was there. It probably was the reunion that ended their affair.

Elvis gallantly took the blame when his romances faltered and he was backed into a corner by the press. He explained how hard it was to carry on a love affair, however genuine, when you're constantly on the run.

"We finally broke up," he said, "because I thought it was the only fair thing to do. I made no fast promises. There were no chains. I told Nita many, many times to date other people. She'd been closer to me than any girl I'd ever known."

Elvis ambled rather than raced through the Hollywood list of available girls in Hollywood in the early sixties. There was Nancy Sinatra, nineteen, who presented him with a gift from her father to commemorate their TV special. They'd known each other before and, as was the custom, columnists presumed that any friendship that went three or four dates meant the couple was engaged. If there was any inclination on the part of the press to make a "thing" of their new meeting, Nancy spooked them quickly by announcing her engagement to singer Tommy Sands.

Nancy Sharp was supposed to have bowled Elvis over—an uncommon accomplishment. Elvis was cool when it came to letting others know where his interests lay. She was a luscious blonde, tall and slender, who'd done some singing in her native St. Louis but switched careers to costume design, ending up in Hollywood as a junior wardrobe mistress when she met Elvis. He was filming *Flaming Star*.

Noticing Nancy Sharp wasn't exactly difficult. Her good taste stood out in the outfits Elvis saw floating around the studio—girls in hot pants and tight sweaters. Nancy stayed with simple ensembles suited to her work—and her breeding. She wore blouses, skirts and comfortable shoes.

Elvis persuaded her to accompany him to Memphis over a Christmas holiday, making no pretense that it had been an easy job. Nancy had promised her family to spend the holidays with them, but she finally succumbed to Elvis' pleas and visited her family briefly en route.

After the Memphis trip, the Presley-Sharp pairing ended abruptly. The pattern was familiar. Hollywood's likeliest and loveliest girls figured briefly in Elvis' life, flaring up like comets, filling him with excitement and the girls with anticipation. Then the friendships flickered out and only their names were entered in the record book.

Juliet Prowse, generally regarded as a special girl friend of Frank Sinatra, landed on Elvis' "Don't call again" list when she hinted that Frank was sore at her friendship on the set with Elvis.

Then there were the beauty queens, Linda Thompson and a former Miss Georgia, Diana Goodman. Plus how many others whose names never appeared in print?

There were various explanations why Elvis' affairs gave him a reputation as a hit and run batter who never made it all around the bases. Some felt it sprang from the upbringing of his mother. Though she was interested in her son's success, she was still a country woman who hoped that one day Elvis would settle down. Elvis was determined to live up to her expectations. He was influenced by her old-fashioned attitude that marriage was a life-time contract.

His feelings were so strong in this respect that, for a time, his father's second marriage to Mrs. Davida Dee Stanley, a divorcee, troubled him. Elvis regretted what he recognized as lack of maturity but it was one of those things he couldn't control. Eventually "Dee" won his heart—by not attempting to be a stepmother or trying to take Gladys' place in his heart. That, she knew, would have been impossible. Dee became his friend and a very good one.

When someone asked, on seeing Elvis surrounded by his adoring family, the *Memphis Mafia* and the odds and ends of chums who gathered around him regularly either in Hollywood or Graceland, "How can a man be lonely with all that company?"

"He's looking for something," said a girl who knew Elvis rather well during his Army stint in Germany. "Looking for something or someone. But I don't think he even knows it himself, only it's a lot harder to look with a lot of people always looking over your shoulder."

"And what is he looking for?"

"Well, being an only child, he was always lonely," said his father, Vernon. "He got along swell with the other kids when he was little—but I always had the feeling he was kind of lonely, and that's kind of odd when you think of all the people around him today..."

Elvis both contradicted and confirmed his father's view in a comment made shortly after his mother's death: "We were always an affectionate family," he said. "My mother was the most wonderful person you could imagine. I can't tell you. I don't know words to make it clear.

"I was always a little bit lonely, maybe a better word would be incomplete, when I was little. But I could tell my mother about it, how I felt, and she'd talk to me, and then the feeling would go away.

"I suppose it might have been different if my brother had lived. A lot of things might have been different. But he didn't live, and I grew up alone. I guess my mother—and my father too, of course, were trying to make up for that by giving me enough love for two."

That was the only time Elvis was known to talk about his twin brother.

*   *   *

Perhaps one reason Elvis' glamorous Hollywood guests in Memphis took second looks at their friendship with the star was their surprise—perhaps a little shock—at discovering that a young lady out of his past had taken up residence in Memphis, occupying an unusual role in Elvis' life when he came home to Graceland.

The very first Christmas that Elvis spent in America as a civilian, his house guest was Priscilla Beaulieu. Her father's position in Frankfurt kept the two apart, so it was agreed that she would come for the holiday, and if the arrangement suited everyone, the pretty, dark-eyed brunette with the wide mouth and engaging smile would live with the senior Presleys, Vernon and Dee. Priscilla attended high school in Memphis and that was the last the public was to hear about her for the next seven years.

Priscilla seemed to have been hidden away within the walls of Graceland, receiving little attention from the outside world, although Elvis always came back to her after finishing a movie or one of his road tours.

Behind this mystique lay the fine hand of Colonel Parker who wanted the quiet relationship between Elvis and Priscilla kept quiet. The Colonel believed Elvis, besides being a superstar, had become America's favorite topic of gossip. The more mystery that surrounded Elvis the more talk and speculation he would invite.

It was an old view belonging to Hollywood of the silent days, but, in so many ways, Elvis was a throwback to the stars the public thought they knew everything about but actually were aware of very little. They were parcelled out gossip in its purest form—half truths and wild fabrication. It made for provocative reading and provided Elvis with a dimension of desirability that matched his obvious sex appeal.

Priscilla had become Elvis' protegée, the attractive, innocent high school girl he would carefully mold into an attractive, sophisticated young woman. She was not permitted to cut her shoulder-length hair until Elvis decided she was old enough. Priscilla offered no childish objections. She was simply in love with Elvis and whatever he asked suited the girl perfectly. Priscilla had been in love with him since she was fourteen, and nothing had happened to change her affection.

Elvis always maintained that when he married he would live in Memphis and any trips to Hollywood would have to be considered as visits. "Anyone I marry," he said, "will have to understand Memphis and like it, because that's my home."

In a six-year span, Priscilla had matured into a woman. Elvis, more than anyone else, was responsible for her look, her attitudes and her interests. Everything she'd done and learned during these most important years of her life had been accomplished to please him.

In the same years Elvis had matured too. He'd finally become reconciled to his mother's death, accepting the tragedy as part of a larger plan for his life.

With the passing of anguish, he'd also come to realize that no woman could be Gladys Presley, but that some other woman might also be ideal—embodying the qualities of a perfect wife and mother. These were the traits he found in Priscilla, and he was determined not to lose her, as he had so many girls, either through his own rigid standards or an inbred distaste for the modern career woman, the career-conscious stars he played around with in Hollywood.

*   *   *

While Priscilla was growing up in Memphis, Elvis was back in the limelight. After making his splashy return via the Sinatra *special* and *G.I. Blues*, he moved into the ranks of the most popular entertainers of the sixties. He'd changed. Gone was the intensity that characterized past performances—the excitement and the passion.

Elvis was no longer a vibrant, pulsating young singer but rather a pleasant, easy-going guy. In that respect the life of an actor suited him. Live performances became fewer and he began devoting most of his energies to the camera. Elvis hoped to become a good actor, and in many respects he was. Elvis was convincing enough in the tailor-made characterizations of the more than two dozen films he made. He played a wide variety of roles, a pilot, a racing car driver, a skipper, a doctor, a trapeze artist and, of course, he portrayed a young singer trying to get a "break" more often than he cared to remember.

How hard Elvis tried to be a good actor was evident in the story that when he reported for work at the start of *Love Me Tender*, he not only had memorized all his own lines but everyone else's as well.

He photographed handsomely in color and few stars on the screen in the sixties matched Elvis in looks and sex appeal. The heyday of tough young men with crooked noses and cauliflower ears had come full cycle, so Elvis, by default, remained one of the relatively few male stars women could sigh over as they had in earlier days when Tyrone Power and Robert Taylor represented the epitome of masculine attractiveness.

The sixties were different from the fifties for Elvis as well as the rest of the world. Music was the way to communicate and more and more people with something to say were picking up guitars and singing. For Elvis, it was time to stand aside and to concentrate on what interested him most—films.

Yet his name commanded as much attention as ever. Two separate instances show that Elvis was never in any slump. His concert fans still adored the Presley name, and they could hear the *Presley Sound* on records. Finally, they could meet him on the screen.

Elvis and the Colonel arranged for the star's famed gold Cadillac to be used as a charity fund-raising attraction all through the world. The car's first stop was Sydney, Australia, where over a quarter of a million dollars was raised. It all went into the charity chosen for the benefit. It seemed wild! The very idea of people flocking to an exhibition—just to see an Elvis Presley car!

Elvis' original guitar, used in recording such hits as *Heartbreak Hotel* and *Hound Dog* was requested for exhibit at *Expo '67, The World's Fair* held in Montreal, as part of the Popular Music display in the American Spirit Pavillion.

The sixties became a mellow time for Elvis,

although he was torn between his desire to run free with his friends and to settle down. It was a nagging debate which took a long time for Elvis to settle—and then it ended in disaster.

* * *

For many years Elvis ran back and forth between Priscilla and the *Memphis Mafia*, who had been located in various homes around Hollywood. He was eager to establish roots in Tennessee. But he continued to be divided between the desire to settle down and his desire to run free with his friends.

The *Memphis Mafia* has come under a great deal of criticism since (and before) Elvis' death because of a book written by a group of discontented employees titled *Elvis, What Happened?* It came as a shocker—and an incredible best-seller—onto the stands, painting an entirely different picture of Elvis from that which the public knew and loved.

Whatever they are called, entourage, in former times, *gofers*, stooges, sycophants, muscle men, bodyguards, or hangers-on, the men around a star invariably arouse animosities. Although they have been hired to protect a public personality from intrusion on his privacy, to handle everything from business affairs to arranging a discreet rendezvous, they become victims of two human traits, jealousy of anyone who gets close to their hero and an exaggerated sense of their own importance.

After returning to civilian life, Elvis began surrounding himself with a group of young men who, although visible, became as mysterious and reserved as the star they served. They remained remote from the public, were hard to reach and were drilled in the art of non-communication. Their nickname, *The Memphis Mafia*, was inevitable. If President Kennedy could have his Boston Mafia, Elvis watchers quickly grasped the opportunity to fasten the handle on Elvis.

Elvis explained, "I can't go around always apologizing for being someplace and innocently causing a lot of trouble. This is the way it is. It's like being in prison. I can't go in a store and look around or places like Disneyland that I'd love to see."

So the *Memphis Mafia* managed the chores Elvis couldn't handle personally. They varied in number over the years, in age, experience and in assignments. Red West was one of the first young men to join Elvis. He was a cousin, a sandy-haired six-footer raised in Memphis. A broad-shouldered youth was Alan Fortas, another friend from Memphis who was the nephew of U.S. Supreme Court Justice Abe Fortas.

Elvis and Joe Esposito became friends when they were buddies in the Army. Joe visited Elvis in Memphis and he joined the group. Joe, who became Elvis' road manager, brought a different tone to the virtually all-Southern contingent. He was from the north, with a Yankee's respect for briskness, efficiency and punctuality.

The young men around Elvis varied in number from time to time; sometimes there were only a few, often there were twelve. Elvis explained his need for the group. "When I move around, someone has to handle the luggage, another takes care of the travel arrangements. We need a good bookkeeper. We're like a business on the move. You couldn't possibly handle it all by yourself."

He was right and top stars sympathized with him. Elvis was a road show—a big production even if it contained only one star. Whether they're called *Memphis Mafia* or *Entourage*, the people surrounding a star become so totally involved in the life of one person that they lose their own identities.

Moreover, the star, unwittingly perhaps, takes outrageous advantage of them. A man running a business knows how many hours of work he can expect from an employee. A star presumes his flunkeys will be on duty day and night. They're expected to anticipate his moods, his mercurial disposition, his eating habits. They're supposed to tolerate all his eccentricities and most of all, they are required to be loyal.

It is a nerve-wracking, ultimately demeaning job. The rewards are consistent with the star's generosity. Cheapskate stars are the rule rather than the exception. No one could have been more generous about his *gofers* than Elvis.

He showered them with every gift imaginable—cars, cuff links, handsome wardrobes, rings. They lived well and besides living expenses they were paid salaries that varied according to their job classification—from a hundred to two hundred dollars a week. One star complained, "A guy like Presley ruins it for us poor suckers who've travelled the world with a single valet or dresser. Now they want 'staff' to help them out."

For the star, the dangers of depending on his entourage are vastly more dangerous. He has no longer hired "staff." He is no longer the boss, but the idol of a "group of friends." Theirs is the company he seeks out when he's troubled. The boys rub his back when his body aches. They comfort him when his romances go sour. They tell him his performance was great—even if reviews scream otherwise. It becomes a vicious circle to which there is no alternative but to shift staffs at regular intervals, avoiding over-dependence, or worse, familiarity. That it breeds contempt is shown over and over again in Show Biz annals, now in politics and in the lives of all the *Beautiful People* whose private lives have become the *literary rights* of their servants.

*　　*　　*

Of course, the main concern of the *Memphis Mafia* was to insure Elvis' privacy, especially when it came to the girls he'd like to meet and those he sought to avoid.

It was a 'round the clock job, but the boys never seemed to mind. Elvis had found a luxurious pad in Bel Air which he had fixed up with electronic gadgets he doted on, closed-circuit TV, enclosed behind a wall that had enough protective devices built into it to discourage any intruder.

The action really got hopping at the Bel Air pad the minute Elvis wrapped up the final shots of a movie and knew he wouldn't have to face the early morning calls which he dreaded. If he'd had his way he would have flown directly back to Graceland, but he was required to hang on until it was reasonably sure there would be no need for retakes.

"Once those early morning calls are behind me," Elvis said, "I feel like a bird who's just been let out of his cage and wants to fly a little. I want to flap my wings. I want to feel sure I'm free again. I never know what I want to do, but I sure want to do something that has nothing to do with the business."

That was the signal for the pad to fill up with girls, old friends and new ones. After finishing one of his flicks, Elvis was in a "loose mood." Someone asked if he might invite a certain girl to Elvis' house. Elvis shook his head, "You know she's a bad one. You never know what she's going to do next. Why don't you stay away from her? She always spells trouble."

The pal was about to pull back, but Elvis switched abruptly, "All right, bring her along, if it's going to make you happy." The girl arrived and Elvis had forgotten his warning.

The party was going along fine. There was singing and dancing and everybody seemed to be having a good time—except this one particular girl.

Nothing seemed to please her. For a long time Elvis' pal tried everything he could to bring her out of her shell and into the fun. But it was all wasted effort.

Finally he put his arm around her and said, "Come on, let's dance."

Suddenly she grabbed at her purse and pulled out

a small knife. "Damnit, don't touch me," she yelled. "Don't you dare touch me! Don't put a hand on me! I didn't come here to be with you. I came here to be with"—she pointed at Elvis—"him! I know he doesn't want me, but no one else is going to touch me."

The party stopped cold. Elvis regarded the shaking girl for a few moments. Then he said, "Honey, we're all here to have a good time. That's no way for a nice girl to act. You're breaking up the party. How about calming down and taking it real easy. Just for me!"

The girl stared at Elvis. Then just as suddenly as she had exploded in fury, she collapsed into a soft lump of uncontrollable tears. She turned to Elvis' friend, "Take me home," she said, "just take me home."

Everyone tried to capture the spirit of the party again, but it didn't work. No one felt very comfortable. Anything could have happened when the girl was in her temper tantrum and wielding the knife. Someone said, "Elvis knew she was a little nutty, and I'll bet he knew she'd pull some kind of crazy stunt. But that's Elvis, always ready to take a chance."

In Hawaii, even the *Mafia* got worried at the way Elvis rode his motorcycle. He was careful in one way, making sure there was no traffic on the hills. But he came so close to going over that he terrified everyone. Elvis had had a number of bad spills with his bike riding, but as long as none of them landed him in a hospital he didn't seem to care.

A young actress who dated Elvis told of an incident: "He said he just wanted to take me for a drive in the country above Los Angeles toward Santa Barbara. I almost refused, as I told him, there were rumors all over the place that he was married to Priscilla. But he told me that I shouldn't pay attention to gossip.

"Anyhow, we took off in his car early the next afternoon with a couple of his friends on motorcycles behind us. I expected see some of the countryside with a beautiful man beside me!

"But for the next three or four hours all I could think of was, would we get out of it alive. Elvis really drove that automobile. I couldn't do a thing but hold on. Elvis sure loved my screaming when we took the curves. He grinned like a devil. You know, I'm convinced he had so much fun driving he doesn't remember who the girl was who was with him.

"One thing struck me on the way home. He was very silent. He drove carefully and when he said good-bye he looked tired—very tired."

Elvis' "tired look" was the source of many rumors and probably they all had a bit of truth to them, that Elvis' health wasn't being watched as carefully as it should. He'd almost choked to death on a capped tooth that lodged in his throat while he was dancing. They got him to a hospital where it was removed. They said doctors wanted to explore further—to make sure no minute scraps were left in Elvis' lungs.

Another source said that the X-rays taken showed symptoms of trouble in his lungs.

Whatever, the studio shuddered every time Elvis

got near a motorcycle or one of his souped-up cars. They worried that he might end up the same as James Dean—a beautiful man who became a mangled corpse by the side of the road.

Someone asked Elvis how he felt about danger, if, like James Dean, he was hypnotized by it, "No," he answered. "I'm not that kind of man. I've got too much respect for life to do anything that might endanger mine or others. Most of those stories people are writing about my 'search for danger' aren't really true. They exaggerate things.

"Everyone likes to get behind the wheel and push a beautiful car as far as it can go. You do that kind of thing once in a while—just to feel what it's like. But I'm no fool. I think I'm as smart as the average guy. I do it when conditions are right, when the road is clear and when I'm clear.

"I think there's a big difference between thrill driving and just pressing a motor to its biggest strength. That's where Jimmy Dean made his fatal mistake. He was driving himself, challenging himself—not the car. I don't worry about me. I don't like suicide.

"Shucks, I'd hate to see my blood scattered all over the pavement and I know I'd live just long enough to enough for that to happen. The sight of blood scares me. Being a G.I. in Germany was enough for me. I don't want any wars in my time.

"Killing's not my sport—not even a poor little jackrabbit on the road. You drive across the country and you see them by the dozens on the highway. It makes me sick. Of course I know people had nothing to do with it. Those critters just run out to the light. And wham! They've had it. I haven't hit more than a couple, but even the thought of that makes me sick."

*　　*　　*

A magazine once collected comments from some of the gals Elvis turned on. Ursula Andress said, "He's a very well-mannered and sensitive person just like me."

Ann-Margret settled everything when she said, "He's a real man."

Mary Ann Mobley said, "He knows how to be a gentleman and he knows a lady when he sees one... He has even more talent than most people realize. He's a natural actor—and that's the best kind of method there is."

Shelley Fabares explained, "He's very intense and has a lot of self discipline. It's wonderful to work opposite somebody you feel really cares about what he's doing, the way Elvis does."

A lot had to do with how Elvis felt about movie making at a given moment. He blew hot and cold about his film career. And who wouldn't under the circumstances? There was never a package put together that extended beyond exploiting Elvis' talents and his name. No one ever came along with a solid story, a real gutsy piece of work that a dozen singing actors could play but to which Elvis might bring an added dimension—his personality. That's the type of story he needed badly but never found.

Continuing the round-up, Tuesday Weld glowed

at the mention of Elvis' name, saying, "We could talk about anything."

Connie Stevens said, "He's naturally kind and thoughtful and good. Best of all, in spite of his huge success, he's unassuming."

Jocelyn Lane paid Elvis the ultimate compliment, "He'd be a tremendous success as an actor, even if he never sang a note."

From Joan Blackman came, "As to Elvis' entourage, I got along with every one of them. They were wonderful around me, and any girl who wants to date Presley knows she has to get along with his boys. The trouble is, some girls resent them and want to get Elvis off by themselves."

*   *   *

Not all the girls agreed that Elvis was the equal of his press clippings, a Southern gentleman, yes. Likeable, pleasant and fun-loving—that seemed universally agreed.

One young lady who measured her words very carefully was Marianna Hill, an intelligent young woman, who gave an entirely different impression of Elvis. Looking back at the observations she made more than a decade ago, one wonders if perhaps they'd been listened to, Elvis' tragic death might not have been averted.

It certainly wasn't on Marianna's mind. Elvis was at the height of his fame. But clearly she had perception and an analytical mind that some of the other girls who knew Elvis or appeared in his pictures with him didn't possess.

Marianna Hill played opposite Presley in *Paradise, Hawaiian Style* and, like so many girls who worked with the Rock star, she'd looked forward to the event with delight. Elvis and a new leading lady didn't really have to go as far as Schwab's Drug Store to start the gossip columns rolling. But when a luscious girl like Marianna was tucked away with the Sex Symbol in Hawaii, inevitably tongues started to wag.

But Marianna came back from the location with her enthusiasm dampened and her enthusiasm for Elvis decidedly chilled. "It was so beautiful in Hawaii," she told an interviewer. "But it was like being alone in paradise. There was no one to share it with.

"Elvis and his entourage (the twelve boys plus the police guard that stood outside his hotel all night) stuck together. They weren't too outgoing or friendly. They seemed to be on the defensive, suspicious of people they didn't know.

"Under the circumstances it was terribly difficult to be congenial. Every time I said something, the boys seemed to interpret it as meaning I was buttering them up to get to Elvis.

"They expected me to go to them. Well, if you did that, they figured you wanted something from them. When I arrived I wasn't introduced to either Elvis or Colonel Parker. I had to walk up and introduce myself."

Eventually Marianna broke up the boys when she put on black tights, a black leotard and went out on the balcony of her hotel, pretending she didn't know they were watching. She performed a sort of ballet dance and the ice was broken.

Every night after that, when they'd finish working, the boys wanted to know if Marianna intended putting on her dance.

"When I first worked with Elvis he seemed somewhat flirty. He said things I'm sure he's said a lot of times—complimenting me on how small and dainty my hands were."

Marianna turned out to be a pretty intelligent and uninhibited young woman when it came to interviews. She was one of the first of his leading ladies to worry about his eating habits.

"Elvis is a big guy. Over six feet. But he's not in such great shape. In fact, he was putting on weight during the first weeks of filming, so he'd sneak out of the hotel late each night and work out at a gym.

"Elvis loves starchy foods, which accounts for his tendency to gain weight. Things like mashed potatoes and bread. He likes popcorn a lot. He really doesn't eat a balanced diet. Yet he looks young. Too young, I think. He's thirty and his face doesn't look like he's lived at all. There's no maturity, no lines, no muscles in his face.

"He just likes to stay inside and eat popcorn and watch television and laugh it up with the boys. When he finds a girl that interests him, the boys make all the arrangements. Then she goes to the house and they eat popcorn.

"I think Elvis shies away from the public because he's afraid. Not because he's afraid of being mobbed but because he's afraid of showing himself. He thinks he always has to put on a big show."

This extraordinary interview by Marianna Hill, published in *Motion Picture* in 1966, hinted at so many things that were to affect Elvis' future, his relations with women and his marriage.

Miss Hill revealed that there was a big strain of narcissism running through Elvis. "He adored making grand entrances," she said, "even on the sound stage or from his dressing room. You know, Elvis is always competing with his leading ladies. He doesn't seem to want you to get serious with your work because he knows you are better trained than he. So he likes to break up a scene all the time, and that throws you. He doesn't concentrate on what he's doing. He acts as though he cares, but he doesn't."

What dismayed Marianna most was that Elvis never talked about things that were important. For example, although they'd become good friends before the picture ended, he never mentioned Priscilla or his mother. He never spoke to Marianna about Graceland, his place in Bel Air or even about Memphis. She felt that he was reluctant to talk about anything that held a special meaning for him. "He spoke only of the little things. Like the fact that he once went on an all-pink kick. The time he wore nothing but pink and bought a bunch of pink cars."

What surprised her most was Elvis' lack of interest in other people or their lives. She found him too self-conscious and self-involved. But she was inclined to blame this on his position. "Elvis is a show business phenomenon. A business commodity. He sells a lot of records. So I think he feels he has to guard himself from people."

Tony Taylor who did the interview, reported that Marianna's final statement dealt with Elvis and why he never went out. Elvis answered, "Because I got mobbed." Wrote Tony Taylor, "A loud, unmistakable Marianna Hill-laugh came over the telephone as she added, 'Maybe he would—but not by me.'"

* * *

An extraordinary example of how far Elvis would go to keep himself protected occurred when the *Paradise, Hawaiian Style* company returned to the studio after its location on the Islands. If there was any place in the world, Elvis could be reasonably sure of safety and privacy—exactly as he wanted—it would be behind the walls of his own studio.

Still, Elvis suddenly ordered a specially made dressing room. Built to his specifications, it was unlike anything studio carpenters had ever built before—at least in the dressing room line. For starters, it had peep-holes in the door. Not ordinary peepholes, but carefully constructed glass masterpieces so that Elvis could sit inside and observe what was going on around him without being observed himself.

It really wasn't necessasry for Elvis to be his own watchman, because the ivory tower was built with an electric lock—a contraption wired to the door, and it could only be switched open by Elvis who knew where the switchbox was.

But the lock and peepholes were only toys compared to the main feature of the dressing room. That was the *secret panel*. According to a studio carpenter who worked on it, "It was hard to believe that we were wasting time putting that sort of contraption for an adult. But I looked at it this way. We were used to doing nutty things for the stars. God, what they could dream up to ask! Elvis was the little kid who never had very much, so he was enjoying his childhood when he was a millionaire."

Anyhow, the panel, opened by a *secret* switch, opened up a *secret* room where Elvis spent his time between takes.

A reporter muttered, "This is pushing the Garbo bit a bit far. After all it's always been next to impossible to reach Elvis anyway. Some day no one will really care."

That didn't quite happen. Elvis' style of public relations changed over the years. Back in the days when his hip swiveling was a novelty, everyone thought that Elvis' kooky style of living was as original as his gyrating songs and the circusy way Colonel Parker sold him to the public.

People were saying, "He's the most refreshing thing to hit Hollywood since the invention of the swimming pool. Imagine being a movie star who thinks it's more fun to stay home at night than go night clubbing or party hopping! Imagine preferring the company of a bunch of Memphis tough guys to the interesting people Elvis could have found in Hollywood."

"Give him a year or two," was the general consensus. "Wait until his career is secure. Then we'll see what Elvis is really like." But as the years passed, Elvis remained the same. Elusive. When he was in Hollywood, the town saw little of him; he remained hidden away at first in the hotels where his entourage occupied whole floors and later, there was the home in Bel Air.

Louella Parsons once wrote: "The mystery deepens as to what does Elvis Presley do when he isn't actually in front of a camera. Next to Howard Hughes, Elvis is rapidly becoming our leading recluse. He goes from set to home, from home to set. As pleasant as he is to co-workers he never lunches in the studio commissaries or at any of the Los Angeles restaurants.

"As far as industry affairs are concerned, he doesn't show up for premieres but frequently buys blocks of tickets which he gives to members of his crew.

"He is not available for charity appearances. But he wrote out a check for fifty thousand dollars for the new wing at the Motion Picture Country Home which was presented by Barbara Stanwyck.

"He doesn't particularly like visitors on his sets, but he never demands the "closed" sign. When asked to, he'll pose cheerfully (more than some extroverted stars do) with important and unimportant drop-ins on the set.

"Elvis has never been known to have any kind of argument with a producer or director. On the contrary, one of his favorite phrases is 'you know best.' Yet he politely declines any social invitations to their homes or parties.

"His attitude is always polite and courteous, and toward women he shows considerable southern chivalry.

"But what REALLY goes with this million dollar baby?"

Chapter 9

Elvis finally decided that it was time to establish a permanent life style for himself. He realized he'd ducked marriage figuring that because he'd been a bachelor so long he couldn't accommodate to the change. How would a wife fit into his life at this stage? He was thirty-two. How would he feel suddenly having to fit his desires into the pattern of another person's life?

Elvis also feared the emotional involvement of marriage. He'd never doubted the depth of his feelings for Priscilla Beaulieu, but he feared the unique pressures of Show Business might affect the happy relationship they'd enjoyed for so long.

One can take for granted that all these doubts were talked over by Elvis and his aides. And if theatrical history, like world history, repeats itself, the answers that came back to him only added to his confusion. Stars' flunkeys are as reluctant to accept a change in the marital status of their King as a new wife is miffed at the suggestion that good old "Maggie," who was the "perfect housekeeper" for her husband's first wife, has "agreed to stay on."

Elvis wasn't prepared for the open warfare that came after May 1st, 1967, when Priscilla Beaulieu and Elvis were married at the Aladdin Hotel in Las Vegas.

They spent a short but peaceful four days in Palm Springs before returning to Tennessee. Because he wanted to bring his wife to a home of her own, Elvis had bought a 163-acre ranch which he named "The Circle G." It cost 250,000 dollars and was located five miles south of Graceland. In yet another moment of fierce determination to establish roots, Elvis finally bought a house in Los Angeles for the cool sum of 400,000 dollars in order that he and Pris would have a real home in California as well as in Memphis.

The conflict within Elvis regarding his wife and his friends became open warfare between two opposing camps.

The boys were used to surrounding Elvis—to flashing his name, basking in his sunlight—and Priscilla represented a definite threat to their happiness, to say nothing of their fat-cat salaries.

Of course, many women would rather have their husband's male friends as adversaries than a fleet of obliging female secretaries and assistants, but in the end, to Pris, it was all the same.

On February 1, 1968, exactly nine months after their wedding day, Elvis and Priscilla became the proud parents of a baby girl named Lisa Marie. For awhile, it looked as though things would be working out between the young couple. Most of Elvis' friends had been relieved of their duties and Pris was satisfied that she was her husband's real love.

She, in turn, was a patient and loving wife, at her husband's side during all the changes that occurred in his career. Life couldn't have been anything less than hectic when you have a young family and are shuttling back and forth cross-country three or four times a year.

Elvis was averaging three films a year, at one million dollars per, plus fifty percent of the profits. Tom Parker saw to that. And he was partially responsible for the new subdued Elvis—as well as an Elvis worn out from endless movie-making.

By 1968, Elvis was itching to go on live before an audience again, and thanks to NBC, he was contracted to do a Christmas special. It was quite an impressive comeback for someone who had been absent from the television studios for so long. The show earned him one million dollars (by now the only kind of figures he dealt in), and more important, it was a re-awakening of his self-esteem as a performer. He proved to himself and to everyone else that he still had what it takes, and that he had complete control over it.

Rave reviews started pouring in, most notably from critics who had made a bad habit of panning him in the past. His sensuous body moved with the music, as it always had, but this time everyone ate it up. Elvis worked hard to make the show a success; he expanded his repertoire, giving the audiences more than just the hip-shaking classics, such as *Blue Suede Shoes* and *Heartbreak Hotel*. He included soft ballads and tender, spiritual hymns—those he had been weaned on as a child.

After this outstanding performance, it was undeniable that Elvis was, finally, a real and enduring talent. His voice was stronger and more powerful than ever before. He was recharged, filled with a new, deeper soulfulness, a more intense feeling than had characterized his singing years before. It now became the songs entirely unrelated to his films that carried the unmistakable Presley touch—songs that began to skyrocket on the charts, most notably, *Suspicious Minds, In the Ghetto* and *Burning Love*.

Elvis started doing live performances again, touring across the country, playing to sell-out crowds from New York's Madison Square Garden to the Houston Astrodome, giving the fans the concerts they had been begging for for so long.

More important, Elvis not only attracted his older, ever-loyal fans, but new, young people—the same age his first fans had been. There were students, housewives, businessmen, professionals—a whole new cult of Elvis fans.

Elvis also started to play two yearly engagements in Las Vegas. A confirmation of his talent, it assured him that he was an established entertainer, in the same league with Sinatra and Streisand. He had come a long way from those concerts where critics had dismissed him as a fad.

Ironically, just as Elvis' career took such a great swing upward, his personal life started to fall apart. Now that Elvis was on the move again, he resented anything tying him down. And when those chums started filing back into the picture, trouble started brewing at the Circle G.

Between working and playing, little time was left over for Priscilla and her needs, not to mention Lisa's. Elvis was the original man's man and his pretty wife couldn't accept it, although they still loved each other deeply.

They'd been together so long that separation almost seemed sacrilege. Priscilla had been more than a wife to Elvis. She'd been his "ward" in many respects, the kid he "enjoyed watching grow up." As soon as Priscilla was old enough to drive, Elvis bought her a Corvair and then a Chevy sports coupe. She lived in a mansion, enjoyed excellent schooling and her romancer was the sex symbol of all sex symbols. What more could a girl want?

There were times when Priscilla asked herself the same question and came up with a provocative—if negative—answer from the Hollywood viewpoint. There was much more to life than just riches. Gradually, Pris began to realize she'd become Elvis' prisoner and the iron bars of her cage closed in tighter on her after they married. She grew tired of the loneliness of their Palm Springs ranch, so Elvis moved Priscilla and the baby to a home in Bel Air where she could circulate more freely with her friends—the few she'd been allowed to make.

From what we know of the beginning of their marriage, both Elvis and Priscilla tried hard to make accommodations. They began entertaining—in the formal style she preferred which didn't mean evening gowns for the ladies and monkey suits for the men.

Priscilla believed in old-fashioned invitations and replies. That worked fine, but there was little she could do about Elvis' friends dropping in whenever they pleased, expecting her to automatically drop whatever she was doing to become a hostess.

The social "gig" didn't last long. Elvis reverted to his old habits, hanging around, doing nothing between engagements, calling his chums in to watch TV. Elvis gave Pris the unmistakable impression that he was bored at home.

By the same token, Pris was bored when Elvis was off on tour. She made up her mind that one way or another she'd have to make a life for herself, if only to preserve her sanity. Elvis' life style was great when they were younger, and she didn't know any better. He was her idol, dream prince, friend—all rolled into one.

But unfortunately her romanticized picture of Elvis was not a fairy tale. She could not wave a magic wand and turn her *Dream Prince* into a *Model Husband*.

Elvis resented Priscilla's ambitions. She'd talked of being an actress, but he would have none of that. "If I wanted to marry an actress, I could have done it a thousand times," he told her.

But could he?

It's an interesting question. In every sense of the word, Elvis was a "catch," from the time he began playing country in the south. He was good-looking, vibrating with talent. He possessed a sense of humor, enjoyed a good time and flashed money with a free hand the minute he laid his hands on it.

Success hadn't gone to his head. He hadn't lost his manners, acquired none of the arrogance associated with performers in the *Rock 'n' Roll* profession. That Elvis wasn't readily approachable was a matter of logistics, the need to save his energies for the show, to prevent fans and well-wishers from taking advantage of him. A star suffers an awful lot of abuse from his public who feel they're entitled to intrude on his privacy at will—interrupting meals to ask for autographs, barging unannounced into his dressing room. The barricades erected by Colonel Parker and the *Memphis Mafia* weren't whimsical. They were necessary.

Nevertheless, Elvis' record with women had been mercurial. He'd never gone with one girl steadily for any period of time although, like Barbara Hearn, they slipped in and out of his life over a long period of time.

In his personality Elvis was more complex than people imagined. The girls he dated were surprised to find he wasn't a barefoot boy from Mississippi they could mold to their own caprices. He was a Southern boy—with a mind of his own. Perhaps that's why the girls who assumed they'd really made it with Elvis found themselves on the outside looking in. He had the reputation of being a "one-at-a-time and one-a-day" lover.

In 1971 *Look Magazine* took a look at Elvis' private life expecting to find it pretty raunchy. The *Memphis Mafia* had just been organized and they had all moved together into a home in Bel Air. With so many young men and plenty of money available, inevitably there were some wild parties.

A girl who attended the affairs told *Look* that she never knew one boy from the other. "They all looked alike. They dressed alike. They talked alike. But they never really said anything. You were supposed to get to Elvis through them, but it never seemed to work out that way."

Another girl claimed that when she arrived, one of the bodyguards explained the house rules. They were fairly simple; to respond to the attention of any of the men who took a liking to her if she expected a return invitation. She was warned to behave in lady-like fashion. They were only given soft drinks. The girl wandered to the back of the house where she found Elvis on a couch surrounded by a bevy of beauties, each jockeying for position to be closer to the King.

It was anything but the orgy of Hollywood legend, according to the girls who made it to Elvis' "do invite list." One girl said, "It seemed that all they did was sit around and watch television. Sometimes Elvis smiled at a girl. When his eye roamed to another corner of the room, the girl stopped smiling. As far as TV was concerned, it played on and on. No one laughed at the jokes. There were no comments about the entertainment. It was sort of like a 'come as you are party'—at the morgue."

Joe Esposito took charge of arranging for the private dates Elvis had. He found the girl, picked her up, brought her to the house where the only sound was that of the television going full blast. No conversation. No mixing by the young people who were invited. Sometimes, four or five girls hung around the living room of the Presley house until midnight or later, unaware that the King had gone to bed.

The whole picture of Elvis emerging from this particular inspection was that of a hard-working entertainer who enjoyed the company of pretty girls, when he had time for them. Obviously, the boys working for him made out a lot better, grabbing all the kicks, making the most of a good deal while they could. Elvis' reputation as a "one-a-day" man overrated his prowess. He was obviously given plenty of support by his buddies.

The *Memphis Mafia* could make some awful gaffs. One involved Connie Stevens, a lovely who could have said "yes" or "no" without a second thought when Elvis called and invited her for dinner. But Elvis, if nothing else, aroused the curiosity of Hollywood. They could always call it a "once-in-a-lifetime" experience.

But when Joe Esposito arrived in a Rolls to drive Connie to Elvis' home, the lady was miffed and let Joe know it. When she wanted an explanation of why the King hadn't driven himself, Joe muttered "little nothings" in the best professional manner of *gofers,* explaining this was the "usual procedure."

They were the wrong words. Connie Stevens didn't buy the "usual procedure." She was accustomed to being pursued by the town's most eligible bachelors who weren't adverse to performing a handspring or two to get a date with her.

Connie's arrival at the mansion was no different from those of the girls who figured in the *Look Magazine* story. She was escorted into a living room filled with boys and girls, the *Memphis Mafia,* all sitting around the living room watching TV. Elvis was not to be seen.

Dramatically, the walls were parted by an electronic device and out stepped Elvis. It was the nearest thing Connie had seen to a trapeze artist's entrance—all it needed was sawdust on the wall to wall carpeting. Elvis spoke to everyone, while Connie tapped her foot angrily. She hadn't accepted a dinner date with Elvis Presley to become "one of the crowd." Rightfully she expected Elvis' exclusive attention. Finally she got up and demanded to be driven home.

For the King this was something new. Vainly he tried to persuade Connie to stay. She'd hear none of his excuses. Hiding his astonishment, Elvis escorted Connie home and their meetings afterward were polite but cool.

*   *   *

Anyone who's ever heard the old smoking-room jokes realizes that country boys don't come to the big city to learn the facts of life. Traditionally, they arrive singularly equipped to cope with the "sexual temptations" of the Big Town. Anyone as obviously sensual as Elvis had little to learn when it came to

166

"making out."

Girls and grown women made him a star. They felt the impact of his good looks and suave personality. They recognized that behind the leer, extravagant costumes, the insinuating voice of a performer who entertained with his whole body, a kid so sexy he had to be shown on TV from the waist up, there lay a sensitive, simple youth searching for the same experiences as they were—love and honest affection.

Elvis went beyond filling their need for a sex symbol. He was a rebel. Yet he was still the all-American boy who loved his mother, country, apple pie and all the things Americans hold dear.

Moreover, Elvis proved the American dream—of the 20th Century. Once every boy knew he could become president. That job having become less desirable, now he knew he could become a Rock Star—just like Elvis Presley, the King who lived like a king and still had a few million left over to pay his taxes and shower pals and strangers with expensive gifts.

No one was ever jealous of Elvis—not even other singers. They didn't envy him either. Elvis had it all—the greatest talent rock 'n' roll has ever known. He worked long, hard and well to earn his title, *The King*.

He could make women shriek and cry when he was up there in the glitter of lights, wearing his jewelled costumes, and dazzling them with his artistry. Yet, in the end, he was a man without love.

167

Until the paternity suit, Elvis had never been involved in a scandal. When he was just a kid, reading the thundering denunciations of the blue-noses, Colonel Parker successfully kept bright the image of a God-fearing, well brought-up young man who neither smoked nor drank and who revered womanhood, even those who tried to tear his pants off when they mobbed him at performances. Elvis' affairs at this stage of his life couldn't have produced more than hit-and-run satisfaction.

When Elvis' Hollywood stays grew longer, there was time to know movieland beauties—from Ursula Andress to Tuesday Weld. Ursula laughed that once Elvis knew she was married, he treated her with the courtliness of a Southern gentleman. Some of his leading ladies he dated; others panted to be asked—and weren't.

The stories his girl friends brought back from their dates played like a broken record. One young lady, who'd been thrilled by a bid to Presley's famous Bel Air pad, could only recall that, besides herself and Elvis, there were only two other people in the room during dinner. She claimed, "It was so quiet I could hear myself chew."

But there was always a woman around when Elvis needed one. Connie Stevens couldn't stay angry long after her first feisty encounter with Elvis. Elvis got over his pique with Ann-Margaret, who told reporters in London that she and Elvis were going to be married. Who could stay angry at Ann-Margaret? They became dear friends. Laurie Goodwin who

168

appeared in *Girls! Girls! Girls!* said there was no romance with him. "We became very good friends. He was very big-brotherish to me. I learned an attitude of relaxation. It helped me keep my balance. I owe a great deal to that alone.

"Elvis was really a shy person. He would feel more comfortable if I were behind the camera when he was singing or dancing."

An old boy friend of Laura's was giving her trouble. One of Elvis' boys was dispatched to the fellow and told him to cool it. Laura appreciated the "protectiveness."

Over and over we have this picture of Elvis, the big brother, the gallant gentleman who doesn't fool around with other men's wives, who becomes a big brother to a nervous starlet.

When, then, did *Elvis, the Wolf* come out of the forest?

Priscilla must have wondered herself as their marriage began to deteriorate. In a different period of their lives, the only girl she'd been really jealous of was Ann-Margaret, but she was comforted by Elvis' assurance that he wasn't interested in a movie star as a wife. Yet they made a fabulously sexy team in *Viva Las Vegas* and to this day, fans maintain their love scenes were on the level.

Of all the stars who drifted in and out of his life, before and after Priscilla, Ann-Margaret appeared to have been the most durable. That was one of the things that went wrong. Priscilla kept reading reports that Elvis was seeing this old girl friend and that one. Names like Ann-Margaret may have been conjured up out of his publicity biography. On the other hand, "Where there's smoke, there's . . ."

One thing was clear. Elvis' old rebel instincts came back with a bang after his marriage. He missed his freedom, his bachelor days and Rona Barrett pinned it all down months before it happened when her adroit reporting figured out all the angles.

Wrote Miss Barrett, "The latest rumble from the rumor factory says that all may not be well with Elvis Presley and Priscilla. Despite the fact that people reported to us that Elvis and his bride were very companionable in Hawaii not long ago, there is other evidence to suggest it may all have been an act."

Then Miss Barrett proceeded to run down what she called the "circumstantial evidence."

Elvis had asked a real-estate broker to look for a six-bedroom apartment in Beverly Hills. The *Memphis Mafia,* who had disappeared after his marriage, slipped quietly back into his life.

Priscilla, still unrecognized by the Hollywood crowd, had been taking in the discotheques, and Elvis, Rona said, was perturbed that she had been spending so little time at home with their daughter, Lisa, leaving the child in the care of a mini-clad governess.

In the daytime Priscilla was taking jazz lessons from instructor Steve Peck. Rona probably deliberately overlooked reporting that the energetic young woman was also deep into karate lessons with Mike

Stone, a champion. The suggestion came from Elvis who was worried about her safety. Threatening letters were never new to him, but lately they had come at a faster rate than usual and he felt obliged to turn them over to the authorities.

Elvis never doubted Priscilla's faithfulness, despite a report by one of the *Mafia* that she'd been seen leaving her dance instructor's home at the small hours of the morning. Elvis refused to believe this.

But when rumors popped that there was something more than karate chops between Priscilla and Mike Stone, Elvis took pains to check them out.

They were true and Priscilla, in a face-to-face encounter announced that she was in love with Mike and intended leaving Elvis. He could barely believe his ears. But Priscilla had had it with the long years of solitude, the months of waiting at home for Elvis to return from his tours. And lately, she had had her fill of stories about his affairs with other women. She was walking out. That was it—flat and final. She flew to Hawaii with Mike Stone.

Elvis and Priscilla separated in 1972, and a divorce was granted a couple of years later after some acrimonious debates between their lawyers about a property settlement. Priscilla's attorneys claimed she'd signed a settlement agreement, unaware of California law which divided all community property equally between the partners in a marriage.

After the divorce proceedings they left the court arm in arm, Elvis proclaiming his continued love for

Priscilla, regretful that his work had led their marriage toward rocky shoals. They would share the love of Lisa Marie—as well as their own friendship, he told newspaper reporters.

For all the facade of friendliness Elvis presented in public, privately he was bitter and hurt. Most of his anger sprang from the realization that he had lost his wife to another man.

It was a bitterness that really never went away.

Chapter 10

Elvis and Priscilla were married in 1967. Lisa Marie was born the following year. She is ten years old now. Like any child who lost her father at an early age, she is going to be asking questions about him for a long, long time, especially from those who knew him—or even were part of the audience at a particular performance.

Like the rest of us, Lisa will be fascinated with the early Elvis, the kid from the south whose rock 'n' roll shook up a whole society in the fifties. She's sure to wonder and will probably be amused at the mentality of those who shuddered at Elvis' sultry, sexy style, his swivel hips and extraordinary vocal agility—the thrills he gave audiences; the shock waves he produced in ministers and pressure groups who growled, "We must protect our daughters from the Elvis Presley exposure."

The "sick" people were those who "discovered" Elvis' "vulgarity"—not the kids who had a nicer way of explaining their love for him. "Elvis turned them on." He was singing to them and for them—telling them the way it was, reminding them it was time to wrap up the past and "do their own thing."

If he'd stopped a second or two in his songs to yell, *Repent, The Time Is At Hand,* maybe he wouldn't have seemed such a "wicked young man" and even Ed Sullivan would have been willing to buck the sponsors and photograph him full figure. But no one was very brave in the fifties.

Sociologically, the early Elvis is, therefore, important. His was a fresh voice, a new sound, calling for a little paprika in the bland world around him. He was a *child* of the Depression and all the repressions he'd endured during those unhappy years came bursting forth like a bolt of lightning bottled up in one of those Mason jars that used to hold *corn likker*.

Professionally, Lisa Marie can find no more exciting period in her father's life than those beginning the year she was born. Her father had been a star for thirteen years, enjoying one triumph after the other. But even the greatest meet bleak spots in their careers.

Talent is elusive; sometimes, an intangible difficult to describe. Putting Elvis into words has never been an easy job either for his audiences or detractors like the arrogant TV reviewer of the New York *Times* who raked him relentlessly with phrases torn from the pages of the *Critics' Handbook of Clichés*. You have to be a pretty tired man at the typewriter to come up with a phrase as unoriginal as: *"There was nothing morally reprehensible about his (Presley's) performance, it was merely awful."*

Elvis had read similar comments over the years.

No one suggested that he leaped with joy when he opened newspapers and magazines to find out how "horrible" he was, Elvis never quite reached the Liberace stage of "laughing all the way to the bank." He left that to Colonel Parker.

As his thirties grew closer, Elvis realized he couldn't continue the juvenile movie type he'd been playing; there had to be a change of pace. It wasn't going to be easy because celluloid is a relentless image maker. Film sticks in the memory, explaining why so many actors become type cast, even strong, dominating personalities more experienced if not more skilled actors than Elvis.

Elvis had terminated his long association with Hal Wallis, moving over to Metro-Goldwyn-Mayer, the once magnificent hallmark of Hollywood elegance. Now, it was shooting movies on short schedules with producers supervising pictures who years earlier wouldn't have been allowed on the lot without a pass from the gateman.

Kissin' Cousins was filmed in seventeen days, produced by Sam Katzman and released by Metro-Goldwyn-Mayer. It was a typical Katzman, true to the style of a man who'd served long and honorably as a B picture producer who in his time had done wonders with low budgets and brief schedules. But was a Presley movie the right vehicle for Katzman to demonstrate his skills?

The musical numbers were literally thrown in without adequate rehearsal, and it showed on the screen. The camera's eye told Elvis' fans they were being cheated. *Cousins* began the slump in his movie career. The film came in two days over schedule but still on budget. The Colonel had gotten Elvis a million dollars for the job.

Elvis teamed up with Katzman again for *Harum Scarum,* playing a singing movie star who helps out the king of a mythical Arab country. It was a muddled story, but it poured another million into the till plus fifty percent of the profits and ended up touring the country as part of a double bill with *Ghidrah, the Three-Headed Monster.*

While it was filming, Colonel Parker suggested the insertion of a scene with a talking camel. It could have been one of his jokes or a serious idea. No one thought of it until after the film was completed. Then they agreed the dromedary would have helped.

Why had the mighty Elvis descended to the level of a *Poverty Row* star? The answer, of course, lay in all that loot. How were the pictures made in such short time and low budgets? By improvisation and thinking of them in terms of "made for TV" productions where the schedule is held down by a minimum of sets, a handful of supporting actors and a no-nonsense director who lets the boners lie where they fall, avoids retakes and keeps players and crew looking so busy that the producer is afraid to come on the set.

The plots of these musical clinkers were largely fantasies, shallow and skimpy, allowing some substance to show before leading Elvis into a song or what passed for a production number. Elvis had become indifferent to the music. Before production started they'd send the script and proposed songs to

Memphis for Elvis to look at. He seldom bothered, arrived on the lot and did whatever was asked of him.

It was just another job and he began to loathe it—especially since he believed what others long had said about him. Given the right material, Elvis could have been a first rate actor. "Show me a good singer," said Frank Sinatra, "I'll show you a good actor. A singer needs presence. Presley's got it."

Veteran Joe Pasternak who did a couple of films with Elvis had enormous respect for his talents. But like other producers assigned to the "last Presleys" Pasternak knew what he was expected to do. Turn it out fast and cheap. If everything else failed, the soundtrack album usually sold well—especially if they threw in retreads of Elvis' old records.

Elvis knew what was happening to him and felt keenly about it. An English publication, *Elvis,* produced by teenaged fans in England, announced sadly that it had stopped reviewing their idol's pictures because they'd become nothing more than "animated cartoons."

Who was to blame? The Colonel, of course, and Elvis couldn't plead innocent. He'd grown up since the Colonel first shook hands on a contract and was quite capable of speaking his mind. But by the middle of the sixties, after so many years of filmmaking, the time to take a stand had passed.

The answer lay in a change of pace—taking a furlough from Hollywood, hitting the road again.

*   *   *

Colonel Parker had already taken steps toward pulling Elvis out of his rut. The Colonel's attitude was simple and straightforward. Money wasn't everything; it didn't buy happiness or contentment. He was thinking of Confederate money, of course.

To buy what Elvis needed, he arranged an elaborate deal with NBC to star Elvis in an hour-long Christmas special at his going rate—a million dollars. To make the deal attractive, the Colonel packaged it as a show with the film distribution rights thrown in. It was a package no network could resist. It answered doubts that had been haunting Elvis; specifically, how to accomplish a change of pace.

It had been a long time since he'd appeared on TV. This was the Colonel's idea. He was dead set against over-exposure. He'd kept his "boy" in films for almost eight years, turning down the stadiums, concert halls, blandly rejecting a million dollar guarantee from Australia for two performances. Besides Australia, there were the mammouth *Rock Concerts* offering incredible fees for the privilege of watching Elvis perform a wiggle and a half, one chorus of *Hound Dog* and be whisked away by helicopter, protected by the State and National Guard. The Colonel dismissed these out of hand.

In the light of the times, the big money involved in these offers were *fantastic*. No one else was getting them. Today, it's different. A handful of superstars can ask for the moon—and get it. You can have a Brando for six hours at X hundred thousand dollars, Charles Bronson for XX hundred thousand dollars and he'll even visit the producer's office.

Remember, it was the Southern Colonel, Tom Parker, who started it all when he first sat down with Hollywood titans to discuss Elvis' original movie contracts. One leaned back in his giant-sized chair in an office the size of St. Peter's Basilica, twirled his thumbs, and after a quiet moment of introspection, said, "How would twenty-five thousand be for a starter?"

Colonel Parker's answer was as quick as his smile, "Sounds fine. That's good enough for me. Now, let's talk about 'my boy.'"

Elvis' producer for the Christmas show was to be Steve Binder, a man with a fine reputation in the tricky field of *specials*. Whipping a show together with a big star looked fairly easy, but producing one that would collect both ratings and *approval* was another.

TV had learned to become indifferent to reviews, but newspapers had changed with the times. Their television critics had become more keenly tuned to the public's preference in entertainment. They couldn't afford to be superior, forever writing over the heads of readers. They'd become more accurate barometers of what the public would stay *tuned to*. A man like Binder wasn't in business to lose viewers at the half-hour commercial break.

Binder's partner was Bones Howe whose association with Elvis dated back to the fifties when he produced Elvis' records. Binder and Bones had definite ideas of what the show represented in terms of restoring Elvis' waning image. According to Jerry

Hopkins' extremely well done biography of Presley, Binder said:

"The way I felt about it was that the television *special* was Elvis' moment of truth. If he did another MGM movie, he would wipe out his career and he would be known only as that phenomenon who came along in the fifties, shook his hips and had a great manager. On the reverse side, if he could do a *special* and prove he was still number one, he could have a whole rejuvenation thing going."

The two were fortunate in having Bob Finkle as their executive producer who assumed the title of vice-president in charge, keeping Colonel Parker amused and out of everybody's hair. The producers wanted to get close to Elvis, to work with him, bypassing Parker, so they could capture the stimulation of his own crativity as Howe succeeded in doing when they recorded. "People would see Presley as he was—not what the Colonel decided they should see."

No one expected the Christmas *special* to be easy, not with the mercurial personalities involved. A hundred or more people were involved but assuming they were all assembled and allowed to have total control, they could not possibly have created the problems of Colonel Parker. He would have been satisfied if his "boy" just took the mike at the beginning of the hour, sang two dozen Christmas songs and wished his audience a happy holiday. Who knows that he might not have been right?

Ever so slowly Binder and Howe began to get their conception across, an hour show with a slight story line that afforded Elvis an opportunity to sing not only his own songs but those associated with other entertainers. This hurt the Colonel most—right in the pocketbook. It meant Elvis would be feathering the nest of another singer, another recording company, and so on.

Billy Goldenberg came in as musical director, worried that he'd never manage to find rapport with Elvis. His doubts proved groundless. The two men got along famously, and Goldenberg later recalled that the impromptu sessions were sheer delight. He was impressed with Elvis' sense of humor, mostly, his willingness to poke fun at himself. Lots of times Elvis would go into one of his numbers as though he were a Presley mimic instead of the original article.

There were disputes over costumes. In the show Elvis wore black leather for the first time, a step he'd been reluctant to take because he hadn't originated it.

The energy spent on deciding whether Elvis would sing a Christmas song would have powered a dozen skyscrapers in a blackout. Elvis had no fixed thoughts on the matter, but the Colonel was determined his "boy" would end the show with one of the standard Yule hymns like *Silent Night*. Then the camera would pan in and we'd hear Elvis whisper, "God bless you, everyone!"

Binder and Howe were dead set against it, aware, as was virtually the entire television and radio audience since the lifetime of Marconi, that Christmas shows had never, never ended in any other way. They wouldn't dare!

181

Finally, with Elvis' help, it was decided he would end the show with a new song, *I Can Dream.* It turned out a winner—just the finale the show needed.

When the taping began in front of a live audience, Elvis was nervous. "It's been so long," he kept repeating. But his showmanship wasn't dead, just dormant, waiting for the people "out there" to bring it back to life.

The celebrated show, still fresh in many memories, was taped in June and put on the air early in December against such stalwarts as Red Skelton, Doris Day, *It Takes a Thief* and a Brigitte Bardot movie in New York. Elvis was received as though he'd never been away. The show ran away with the ratings.

Most gratifying to the producers, Elvis, and Billy Goldenberg, who had done most of the heavy sweating, were the reviews the show received. *Eye* magazine's John Landau wrote, "There is something magical about watching a man who has lost himself find his way back home. He sang with the kind of power people no longer expect from rock 'n' roll singers. He moved his body with a lack of pretension and effort that must have made Jim Morrison green with envy. And while most of the songs were ten or twelve years old, he performed them as though they were written yesterday."

Record World reported, "It wasn't the old Elvis, trading on the nostalgia of early rock and obsolete Ed Sullivan censorship. It was a modish performer, virile and humorous and vibrating with the nervousness of the times."

The New York Times said that Elvis "helped bring the pop world from illusion to reality" and called Elvis "charismatic."

For Elvis it was time to take the public into his confidence, saying, "I'm planning a lot of changes. You can't go on doing the same thing year after year. It's been a long time since I've done anything professionally except make movies and cut albums. From now on I don't think I'd like to do as many pictures as I've done—almost three a year.

"Before too long I'm going to make some personal appearance tours. I'll probably start out in this country and after that, play some concert dates in Europe. I want to see some places I've never seen before. I miss the personal contact with audiences."

*   *   *

As Elvis himself had done a decade or so earlier, *The Beatles* flew to America, holed up at the Warwick Hotel in New York, not a skyscraper but a modestly storied building where the English quartette were ensconced in suites on the fourteenth floor or thereabouts. Throngs lined Sixth Avenue to look up at the famed Britishers who came to the window, waving and smiling down at their new American friends.

They had been brought over by the same Ed Sullivan who presented Elvis Presley over his own vow never to have the boy on his show. After Elvis proved what he could do rating-wise, Sullivan's options were nil. He either grabbed new talent fast or conceded defeat to his competitors in the variety field.

Elvis had taught *Old Stoneface* a lesson he hadn't forgotten. If he wanted to remain top man, he needed younger audiences. They were proliferating at a great rate in the sixties, the result of the post-war baby boom. They represented an important chunk of the purchasing dollar and spent a larger share of it on entertainment than had younger generations before. Either one catered to them or ended up as a Sunday afternoon "special event."

The *Beatles* made several appearances on the *Sullivan Show,* and the same trick used to exploit Presley's unfilmed pelvic gyrations were employed to sell the Beatles. Tickets to the *Sullivan Show,* impossible to obtain, even if requested weeks in advance, miraculously became available to teen-age groups. Home viewers had a tough time hearing the English importation for all the squeals of the studio audience. It didn't matter. Their ratings were the best Sullivan had enjoyed in many a year. Handicappers had to go back to Elvis Presley to find anything nearly approaching them.

While they were in Hollywood for a show at the Hollywood Bowl, the *Beatles* met Elvis and warm friendships were made. It was the same when, a few years later, another charismatic English entertainer appeared on the scene with a dynamic style of singing that caught the public's fancy—even if it seemed to have borrowed a bit of everybody from Elvis to the *Beatles* with a touch of *The Monkees,* the *ersatz Beatles* who flourished for a time. This was Tom Jones.

Like the *Beatles,* he sought an introduction to Elvis when he played the Coast and because he remained longer in the States, he became a close friend. Like the *Beatles* he urged Elvis to get back into concert work. He wasn't as frank as others who pointedly asked Elvis why he persisted in making such dreadful movies.

Elvis was finally coming to an end of his film work. *Charro* found him as a western hero out to capture a band of outlaws and a stolen cannon. If indistinguishable from any western ever made, of interest to historians is that this was a film in which "Elvis Presley *didn't* sing." His last feature was *The Trouble With Girls* in which he played the leader of a traveling show, a spoof of the Roaring Twenties. Elvis' celluloid valedictory was notable for the appearances of Vincent Price and John Carradine in what amounted to bit parts.

*   *   *

Since the smash hit of his Christmas *special,* Colonel Parker had been negotiating with the International Hotel in Las Vegas which was still under construction, promising to have the biggest of everything. It would be the tallest building in Vegas, boast the largest casino, the biggest swimming pool (containing 350,000 gallons of water), 240 miles of carpeting, a golf course, a convention hall, six dining rooms, twenty five hundred employees and, of course, the biggest night club in the whole wide world.

The cabaret was going to be called the *Showroom Internationale!* The final "e" was important—but what did it mean? If anyone asked, they were told the *Internationale* would also house a thousand slot machines and the reservations desk would be operated by computer.

Figures like these hadn't been bandied around since Hollywood went to Rome for movies like *Ben Hur* and *Quo Vadis.* Show Biz concentrated on *Showroom Internationale* and kept asking what two thousand extra covers meant to the overall Vegas take. What would it do to star salaries already soaring to Mars? They'd long since bypassed the moon. What acts could fill a cave that big once a night? Would anyone dare two shows a night? Ouch! That question was a stinger. Not becoming to the "gentle pall bearers" of Hollywood and Broadway.

Suppose the "e" on the end of the room's name meant that the place was "rigged"—so you could throw a switch and partition sections of it off on slow nights. How fast would it take for news to leak out that the "e" had been thrown on whosis or so-and-so? Fast enough to worry them in Miami and Houston! That was certain. There was little enough playing time for the *superacts.* It was either grab a whole year's gambling money in six weeks at Vegas or audition for a game show on morning TV.

*   *   *

The great Barbra Streisand was selected to open the *Internationale* and everyone yawned when they heard she was receiving a million dollars for the engagement under a complicated financial arrangement that spread the fee over five years. That was not the jolt that came out of Vegas even after Ms. Streisand was greeted by the sourest reviews the town had read in years. Streisand, being Streisand, shaped up and the place "sold out." At least that was the general impression. What really reverberated throughout Show Biz was the price of drinks—*five dollars per!*

This showed how Vegas had changed in the thirty-odd years it had been in business. The lure of the neon-lighted oasis in the Nevada desert originally was its price. Everything was cheaper in Vegas than any other amusement spa—hotels, clubs, cocktail lounges (with shows), taxis, restaurants. Free Western-style breakfast used to be *de rigeur* at all the early hotels. The theory, of course, was that losses incurred in its restaurants and night clubs were compensated for in gambling profits.

That time-honored policy had been tossed into the loser's circle. Anyone with a stake in Vegas, agents representing supporting acts, show girls, the madams of the bordellos operating outside City limits, worried. As if the price hike was not stiff enough, who could possibly follow Streisand?

Stars who could guarantee *five dollars per* were all tied up under exclusive contract to the other hotels. Who did that leave? Dietrich? Mae West? Sally Rand? Pinky Lee? Maybe, Omar Sharif?

Didn't James Caan sing?

Colonel Tom Parker was sixteen years old in 1926 when the twenty-fifth anniversary of the death of Guiseppe Verdi was celebrated with a festival of his works at La Scala in Milan. The great composer-conductor, Pietro Mascagni, could have used young Parker's carnival chutzpah when he agreed to be one of the distinguished conductors participating. He refused to name a fee, saying he would be satisfied by being paid a few Lire more than his rival, Arturo Toscanini.

Mascagni was chagrined when he received a check for the *Lire* equivalent to one dollar and a note from the management of the opera house stating that this represented more than Toscanini had been paid. Toscanini had donated his services to aid the Festival.

When it was announced that Elvis Presley would follow Streisand into the *Internationale*, no one doubted that the Colonel had wangled a dollar more than Barbra Streisand's extraordinary fee. Even if he bargained from behind. It had been sixteen years since Elvis played Vegas, fresh from the *Sullivan Show*. Not a happy time, especially for the bartenders who mixed malted milks instead of pouring champagne.

Elvis Presley hadn't played to a live audience in thirteen years. Moreover, Elvis had slipped badly at the movie boxoffice; he'd been off the charts for some time and was just edging his way back into the record business. Would smart Vegas audiences buy an aging Rock Star? Especially in view of "new breed" entertainers like The Beatles and Tom Jones?

In spite of the doubts Elvis' proposed return to live performing involved, Colonel Parker was able to seduce the management of the *Internationale* into a million dollars plus for the same period of time, number of shows, etc., etc., etc. as Barbra Streisand.

The extra dollar showed up in more lavish living accommodations than Barbra had enjoyed, an extra patty of butter at breakfast, more marmalade, transportation, etc., etc., etc.

What made the Colonel happy, pleased Elvis. After all these years, the veteran was still the *Medicine Man,* the *Wizard of Oz, Merlin the Magician,* or as one film producer described him, "the *Machiavelli of Managers."* Still, being the King money-wise placed an added burden on Elvis—living up to expectations. He reassured himself by realizing that among Show Biz *cognigenti,* as Jimmy Durante used to say, expectations were low. He had no place to go but "up."

Elvis, when he settled into it, was used to hard work. He had no intention of being the King and falling on his face. He dieted, went into training, worked at his karate with Mike Stone, rehearsed his songs for six weeks.

"Rehearsed his songs." Sounds like playing *Chopsticks* a couple of times a week. Elvis put *two hundred songs* through the wringer with his musicians for four weeks in Los Angeles before he moved to Vegas and two more weeks of rehearsal to whittle down the number needed for the show and choreograph his movements—a detail Elvis seldom paid attention to in younger years.

Movies had taught him the advantages of knowing the best position to be in at given points in a number. This was old-fashioned showmanship, tricks that Caruso and Jolson took for granted. They knew the theatres they sang in so well, they could tell the stage manager what board of the stage they'd be on to hit a note they intended to *really* sock over. The days were over when Elvis could finish a number anywhere—even with his back to the crowd.

The monster café was filled to capacity, even with the tables reduced in size and chairs huddled together, barely allowing patrons to breathe in air-conditioned Vegas, the city where there are no windows, no clocks on the wall—nothing to distract from the Vegas sound, the crackling of dice, the clackety-clack of the slot machines, infrequent cries of "jackpot" and the muffled whispers around the roulette wheels and the green velvet tables of the poker games.

But this night there would be a very special sound—a sound that had swept the world many years ago and now its originator was coming back to show all his hundreds of imitators how it was done. Above the clatter of the forks and knives, the waiters mumbling orders, rushing back and forth to serve them, there hung that heavy atmosphere of worry.

Elvis' friends worried, even those who didn't give a damn whether he made a hit or flopped, worried. That's Show Biz—you don't have to love a guy to worry. Worry comes naturally—part of the excitement, one of the intangibles that makes the

190

profession exciting.

Why does the show have to go on? Because there are two thousand people out there paying a hundred bucks a head to see it. Why must the show go on on time in Vegas? Because there are two thousand gamblers out there waiting to escape and get back where they can lose two hundred bucks a minute.

So there was only the briefest of introductions, over a loudspeaker a disembodied voice said, "Ladies and gentlemen, welcome to the International Hotel and the Elvis Presley show with Sammy Shore, the Sweet Inspirations and the Imperials."

The gold lamé curtain rose. The Bobby Morris Orchestra looked like the Bobby Morris Orchestra in tuxedos. The Sweet Inspirations sang their brief medley of show tunes and it was Sammy Shore's time to build the excitement. Sammy was a Presley regular, knew his stuff, aimed his jokes at Elvis and the Colonel, and got on and off fast.

There was a pause and on walked Elvis. They gasped! He looked sensational in a white kid leather jumpsuit with fringed shoulders, beaded streamer belt around his hips. The band was pounding out a furious, *I Don't Care, Baby.* At stage center, Elvis grabbed the mike, hit a pose from the fifties—legs braced, knees snapping and just as he was about to start, the audience stopped him cold. As one, all two thousand people rose to their feet, pounding, whistling, stomping their feet, standing on tables to get a better look. As standing ovations were rated, this had to be one of the biggest.

Wrote W.S.A. Harbinson: "The myth looks

better than he ever looked before...now the audience is predominately middle class and middle-aged, no longer rebellious but playing the system, safe in their money, safe in their own ideas of purity...And there, on the stage stands the highlight of their lives returned to flesh and blood...One hell of a man, truly tall, dark and handsome.

"He kicks off with *Blue Suede Shoes,* charges through *I Got A Woman,* then leans over the mike in that old seductive pose and starts growling from the back of his throat sly, honey-combed come-ons. He works along safe lines...but he does so with a style and panache that comes close to pure magic. Lithe, raunchy, sweat pouring down his face, he moves with the precision of an athlete, the grace of a dancer."

Of all the rock singers who aged, Elvis was the one who kept his grace. The years had ripened and enriched his voice. It was full and big. He was in total control, holding his notes beautifully, never wobbling. Presley could do no wrong that Vegas night—and he felt it.

He closed with *What'd I Say?* and two thousand people were on their feet. Elvis bowed and came back to finish the show as he intended, singing *Can't Help Falling in Love,* which he used to close every show thereafter.

The critics raved. *Billboard* roared: *Elvis Retains Touch in Return. Rolling Stones* called Elvis *"supernatural." Newsweek* reported: *There are several unbelievable things about Elvis, but the most unbelievable is his staying power in a world where meteoric careers fade like shooting stars.*

Back a few paragraphs it was noted that Barbra did business at the *Internationale*. To no one's knowledge they'd never pulled the "e" and partitioned off part of the multileveled restaurant and balcony with its two thousand capacity.

But truth came out after Elvis opened. "We were opening a new hotel," said one of the managers, "and we read all the signs. We figured Barbra Streisand was the hottest entertainment property in the world. She'd just won an Oscar, she had three pictures going, her name was fantastic. Elvis was an unknown stage property. We weren't sure he'd be a draw, but my God! With Streisand they couldn't keep the damned place full. With Elvis it was full, full, full..." Elvis played two shows a night, and they never pulled the "e."

It was a success beyond belief. Who needed the Vegas regulars? Who needed the freebees who came from the East on charter flights as guests of Vegas' hotels? They were the so-called big spenders, whose gambling paid the cost of their courtesy visit. Elvis did without them too. Vegas' overseas telephone operators had never been so busy, directing calls to the *International Hotel* from Europe, Australia, the Orient—all from fans begging for reservations that had been sold out weeks before Presley opened.

Curiously, when it was all put together, Elvis' trip to Las Vegas in that summer of 1969 paralleled the lonely pilgrimage the kid had made many years ago from Tupelo to Memphis. No one knew why, but there was that feeling that Elvis was going to the right place at the right time.

History was repeating itself. The world had been caught up in a wave of nostalgia that was just beginning to be noticed. Who better to bring it to full bloom than the star who invented the fifties—Elvis Presley?

Was Elvis aware of the nostalgia trend? Did the old Colonel raise his nose to the skies, study the clouds as he used to a half century ago on the Midway, wrinkle his nose and mutter, "Not bad for this time of year! Better haul out the *kewpie dolls*—just in case. They're making the rounds again. There's nothing new in this business—just faces. Even the money's still green."

Oh, yes. At the end of the month-long run, the hotel announced that Elvis had attracted 101,500 customers, far more than Barbra Streisand had, and more than anyone else would.

The Colonel beamed.

Chapter 11

After Vegas, there began a fabulous tour of the United States which climaxed in Madison Square Garden, the first time Elvis had played the historic palace of sports, and now the favorite auditorium of Rock stars.

As well it should be. New Yorkers can often do things right. This is the fourth Garden to have been built in the city, the third to be called Madison Square Garden, although its latest location is blocks away from Madison Square.

Its seats are plush and comfortable; the sight lines good from virtually any part of the arena, and Presley dazzled the *Big Town* just as he'd done in Vegas.

He took one look at the Astrodome in Houston and sighed to his men, "This will never work. Let's do the gig and get out." It was an outrageous spectacle just to look at the over-sized arena. There were 44,500 armchairs, enough to fill a hundred movie theatres. They rehearsed for a few minutes to get the feel of the place, and knew instantly there'd be nothing but noise, echoes, no sound at all in some parts.

There was one good reason for accepting the Astrodome date. Ticket prices had been scaled down to a dollar, so even the poorer fans could get in. Moreover, the engagement was important, marking Elvis' first appearance outside Vegas and serving notice that Elvis was back in business.

Elvis gave the ticket buyers their money's worth—in displaying himself, even if it was impossible to perform a great Presley show. He drove several times around the auditorium standing up in a platform of a truck while the sound systems played records that could have been Presley or Chinese children reciting the alphabet. It didn't matter. Colonel Parker collected his million.

Elvis' tour climaxed in Los Angeles at the Forum, containing 36,000 seats, which originally was booked for one show. But the demand for tickets grew so huge that a second show was scheduled. Finally it rose to four. They could have played six, but Presley was due in San Diego the following day, so that possibility was eliminated. Crowds began assembling outside the arena at four o'clock in the morning.

What was remarkable about these concerts was the boxoffice price. They could have sold for twenty dollars, but Elvis insisted that the Forum be scaled to five to ten dollars.

May Mann, unable to obtain press tickets, like virtually all newspaperpersons, obtained a pair from friends and descended on the Forum where she climbed miles of steps, walked through miles of tunnels to end up seated close to the stage. May laughed, "You couldn't find ushers—they were so taken up in the excitement of the day." What pleased her most was seeing so large an audience of young people.

Wrote May: "Sleek as a tiger, dynamic, handsome, loving all of us and clowning, he invented and improvised and did whatever he felt like.

"'Turn up the lights,' Elvis said. 'You can see me. I want to see you.' Girls screamed, 'I love you, Elvis.' One girl rolled on the floor. The girl seated next to me said, 'I can't stand it—him so near.' Later she explained. 'I'm a hair dresser for the movies. I've never seen Elvis before. He's my idol. I know Hal Wallis and Dean Martin and lots of people who could maybe get me to Elvis for a hello. But I couldn't do it, not without preparing myself for a long time before I could undertake such an experience!' She was an attractive young woman, age thirty."

Elvis talked to his audience. He sang spirituals. He introduced his father. He told the people about the documentary he was making, *Elvis, That's The Way It Is*. He said, "It's the best film I've made in ten years. I hope you like it too."

May Mann, who'd seen so much of Elvis off screen, on screen, at home, in Vegas, believed she'd never found Elvis happier or more relaxed. He kept his cool in the face of some far-out situations—a girl kept calling out such impassioned love protestations that Elvis blushed.

When finally it was over, the people didn't want to leave. They thought if they stayed around long enough, Elvis would come back. Not likely—in view of his mind-boggling schedule.

There are no reports that Colonel Parker saw the show—not with so many boxoffices to check, armed guards and security people everywhere to insure the full till didn't tipple over into any but the right hands. His.

Elvis grossed $313,000 a show, surpassing the one-day record set the previous year by the *Rolling Stones,* $238,000. The Los Angeles *Times* wrote: *Elvis' enormous personal charisma, showmanship and excellent voice shows that he is still way in front of everybody else.*

*   *   *

In January of 1973 Elvis aired a live *special, Elvis, Aloha from Hawaii,* which was sent by satellite to forty countries around the world. It was a benefit on behalf of the *Kui Lee Cancer Fund.* Elvis paid all the expenses, paid for his own hundred dollar ticket to attend the performance and the show was scaled down to $2.

Professionally Elvis was at the top of the world. The Hawaii program set records—as Elvis' performances always did. But divorce clouds were hanging over his head. As he was singing his heart out, making plans for tours of the Orient, Europe, Australia, all the places that begged to see him, the King knew loneliness as he never had before.

His following was stronger than ever, yet he was far from elated, for he had failed as a husband.

But the single life always had its appeal for him, and it served, in the end, to make him more at ease. Too many critics fall into the trap of playing up the loner in Elvis. In his later life, nothing could be farther from the truth. He was constantly surrounded by his admiring and loving friends, doing what made him happy. Since his days at Hume High, he had overcome his childhood fear of peers. And, if nowhere else, his happiness certainly showed in his performances.

And yet some of those friends—or perhaps ex-friends—insist that the only happiness may have been in his performances. As one ex-bodyguard, close to him put it, "He was the loneliest man I ever knew."

All the same, lonely or not—or perhaps because he was lonely—he began playing to live audiences in earnest. He divided his time between national tours and Las Vegas. The reviews from a recent performance, last December at the Las Vegas Hilton, proves that Elvis was still the king: ". . . he went into a mixed bag of new and old songs with a vocal quality and power that far surpassed anything heard from him before." And to add to his triumph, daughter Lisa Marie, now nine, was with him—and the relationship was close.

But there were already signs of the battles he had fought—battles he was still fighting—in his face. There was the weight problem he had fought—sometimes losing weight maybe just a little too quickly, other times hiding the extra pounds in flashier, fancier jumpsuits of sequins and studs and embroidery. There was no way he could hide the fights he'd had with death—the loss of his mother.

He'd certainly had to fight the loss of his wife. But he had lost none of his incomparable talent, his ability to hold and dazzle and thoroughly captivate his audience in a way that no one could—or can—ever hope to touch.

Throughout his career, Elvis had a one-to-one relationship with his fans. No kind of scandal or embarrassment diminished him in their eyes. He was their king—half-saint, half-sinner—the best of both worlds combined.

When everything else had failed, when his friendships with the famous *Memphis Mafia*—his life-long cronies—began to dwindle, when he found himself more happy in his own company than the company of a girlfriend, he still had his fans and his career.

* * *

There were two more girls who played serious roles in Elvis' life. Linda Thomson, whom Elvis met in 1972, and Ginger Alden, whom he introduced on his last TV special as his "girl friend." At the time of his death, Elvis and Ginger were working out a wedding date.

Linda impressed Elvis because she was religious and not given to the sort of language he'd had to become accustomed to around night clubs and movie sets. Success hadn't swollen Elvis' head or changed his moral values. He was still a shy person.

He never undressed if anyone else was in the room and was particular in his tastes in women.

He could sometimes find himself in a bizarre situation—as well as creating a crazy one for a girl he happened to think of. It was nothing for him to be driving somewhere down south, remember a girl he'd met in Seattle, stop the car, call her up and invite her to join him. Whatever the poor girl expected never turned out as magnificently as she imagined. It was a quick shot, a twenty-four hour date, and she was rolling back to wherever she came from.

Linda and Elvis met at a party in Memphis where they were quickly brought together by their background. Linda read the Bible every day, and Elvis was thoroughly familiar with it, even if he was not quite so devout.

He lavished Linda with magnificent gifts and she traveled with a movie star's wardrobe. She was quite different in her attitude toward Elvis than Priscilla. Unlike Priscilla who wanted a life of her own, Linda stayed close to her man. She enjoyed the camaraderie she found in the *Memphis Mafia*, thoroughly enjoyed touring and the helter-skelter life of the road.

Linda was a smart bird. She knew there were times when Elvis preferred to be alone. She slipped quietly away, letting him know exactly where he could find her. As soon as she was out of sight, Elvis wanted her back. And there she was. She stuck around.

The two women were much alike physically.

Linda and Priscilla were both dark, long-haired beauties with sultry eyes and lips. It was taken for granted that Linda and Elvis were going to marry, but abruptly she disappeared from sight.

Elvis continued to make records, to appear on television and do concerts. But there was a change. The glitter had become somewhat tarnished. The bounce? Harder for Elvis to manage. His voice remained in great condition, and that was the part of his vast entertainment bag of tricks that kept him going. But up on the platform, in the heat and glare of the lights, sweat streaming down his face as he worked, you could see that what looked fun and natural had turned into a job requiring tremendous physical and mental effort.

It was no longer possible to hide that Elvis was suffering from weight and health problems. He was in his forties. It is a pretty common condition. After man reaches thirty-nine, unlike Jack Benny, he moves on to forty and his troubles begin. For some reason, forty has been chosen as the time of life when things get different.

The hearty optimist will tell you that "life begins at forty." The cynic warns, "You're sliding downhill and every day brings you twenty-four hours closer to the grave."

The practical person simply continues what he's doing, knowing you can live only one day at a time; aware that tomorrow's sun will rise either in splendor or behind a mask of clouds; but we have no stake in tomorrow, for it is, as yet, unborn.

Chapter 12

As 1977 started, Elvis scheduled some appearances in the South, but they were cancelled and he entered the hospital. Secrecy was imposed on everyone connected with Elvis' visits to the hospital in recent years, but they'd become increasingly frequent. Word inevitably slipped into the press and no one who had seen him in recent concert appearances could doubt that the singer was suffering from a variety of problems even a layman could diagnose.

What appeared to be fat was actually bloat, and there are many men over forty who suffer the same problem. Elvis' bloat was caused by retention of water in the body. A commonly prescribed remedy is cortisone, which doctors warn produces devastating side effects. Rheumatic patients who have tried it once or twice reject the effects, preferring pain.

Suddenly stories began appearing in the press that Elvis was suffering from a drug problem, that his habits were responsible for his mysterious weight and hypertension problems.

Has anyone ever written reasonably about Show Business personalities either suffering a drug problem or using drugs under careful medical supervision—with the utmost personal discipline? I doubt it. The word "drugs" has such awful connotations that it summons the vilest reactions.

There are two stories in my catalogue of memories I like to recall. The first involves the fabulous Blossom Seeley, whose life and times were filmed by Paramount a couple of decades back with Betty Hutton playing Blossom's part in *Somebody Loves Me*. She was an *avant garde* singer, way ahead of her time in choice of material, a rare stylist who rated second to none when it came to putting over a jazz or rhythm number.

She was notable for her fabulous entrances. Blossom always worked in three, meaning, the full stage was hers. The curtain opened to introduce two pianists and seconds later Blossom appeared, beautifully dressed, charging to the footlights with the energy of a beautiful animal at the starting gate.

"How did I do it?" she laughed. "Easy. I took my position behind the curtains about five minutes before I was to go on. I'd stand there buffing my fingernails with the fury of a girl whose date was waiting in a taxi. Try it and you'll see what it does to your nervous system."

Skip a few years and I found myself in the dressing room of one of the great singing stars of all time, still a big name who can pick and choose her *specials* and other TV appearances and every season or two appears in supper clubs of her own choosing or in the summer theatres.

About an hour before her first show, she reached

into her purse, pulled out a bottle containing dexadrine. She removed one pill and with a special instrument carefully cut it into four pieces, placed them on a piece of Kleenex. She watched the clock. Exactly a half-hour before the show, she took one quarter; at the five minutes call, she swallowed the other.

The second half of the pep pill was saved for the second show. "One Dexy a day," she said, "and only when I'm working. I've seen too much talent go down the drain. My doctor told me this is the way to do it. Remember, I'm out there from fifty minutes to an hour. It's a long time to keep your energy up and hold an audience. You need some sort of stimulation. But once you start overdoing it, kiss your career goodbye—and the rest of your life."

* * *

Rupert Murdoch, the Australian publisher, entered the American publishing scene with a tabloid, *The Star,* which, after a poor start using old boilerplate material that dated as far back as the old *American Weekly* of the Hearst empire, began to take form and became a fairly interesting publication of its type, giving the reigning tabloid, *The Enquirer*, a run for its money in so far as personality scandals were concerned. *The Enquirer* in recent years found a bland diet of human interest pieces more profitable circulation-wise and sustained a more consistent readership than the wild extravagances of its past.

Murdoch had money so when the rumors proliferated about Elvis and the news was deliberately leaked that three of the *Memphis Mafia* had been fired under what they considered unfair conditions, a Murdoch man, Steve Dunleavy, was quick to get in touch with them and put their experiences with Elvis down on tape.

The result has been the book *Elvis... What Happened?* by Red West, Sonny West and Dave Hebler as told to Steve Dunleavy. That it appeared at the time Elvis died created both outrage and curiosity. Print orders of the book, blurbed as "the dark other side of the brightest star in the world" have gone into the millions. Its serialization in *The Star* and *The New York Post* did Presley-type business. Editions sold out.

I had never heard of Steve Dunleavy until the book. I saw him for the first time on television the night of Elvis' death when he appeared on a so-called "discussion program" intended to reflect on Elvis' times, what he meant in the evolution of American music and how the future would treat his work which, unlike stars of other generations, has been generously preserved in records, TV tapes and motion pictures.

Dunleavy seemed totoally uninterested in the proceedings except when he was speaking in his Australian accent. He appeared a pinched, small, uncomfortable looking man who would look for the nasty and find it, even if it was totally wrong.

When it came his turn to say something, he managed, "It was a classic case of too much too soon." You'd hardly call that original, but Dunleavy's next line came as a shocker. In effect he was saying that one had to realize that Elvis was, "to use a regrettable expression, *poor white trash*."

When they describe Australia as being exactly a half century behind America in progress, where outhouses are common on the finest residential streets of Melbourne, they must have borne Steve Dunleavy in mind. The expression "poor white trash" hasn't been common in these United States for at least fifty years.

Joe Klein of *Rolling Stone* had gone to Tupelo and one of the people he talked to was Sara Wiygul and her daughter, Mona. Sara is a school teacher and said she had gone to see Elvis at the Tupelo Fair in 1956. "I don't like the way they're saying now that he came from poor white trash. They were poor all right, but they weren't trash. If they were trash, he wouldn't have gotten as far as he did."

Besides not knowing the difference between "poor" and "trash" Dunleavy appeared to have little respect for accuracy when he slapped together the trio's memories of Elvis.

The following are excerpts from *Elvis,* Jerry Hopkins' biography, bits of conversations he held with the musicians who told him what it was like to work with Elvis:

"Elvis changed the songs each night. Seldom, if ever, were the same ones sung in the same order."

"Elvis amused himself a lot. He'd play a few tricks

on the orchestra. They'd be right in the middle of an orchestrated thing and he'd suddenly skip a verse. On purpose. He's got a thing about being locked in—got to do this verse, that verse—and he'll take a notion he don't wanna do that tonight and so he'll skip one, leavin' them up there playin' something where he ain't."

"He didn't do it much, but if he gets a little bugged or something not suitin' him, he'll just kind of drop that show completely and move on in a different direction and start really wingin' it. He threw a few surprises on us."

"He's a strict showman and he really grooves on what he's gonna do. And he really pays attention to his songs and...checks their reaction...You can tell there's somethin' really buggin' him because he can't keep it movin' like he really wants to. But, boy, when he gets it, you can tell it too. He's happy and really lets it fly."

According to *Dunleavy and Company* he some-times forgot the sequence of songs, and he would forget the lyrics to songs. Other times there were songs scheduled to be sung, and he would just refuse to do them.

Dunleavy must have been a pretty naive newspaperman to find anything new in this "sordid" tale of a singer who couldn't remember lyrics or forget the sequence in which they'd been arranged.

In *Rolling Stone* Greil Marcus said that reading

the book hadn't affected him one way or another. It was, he inferred, the type of piece any disgruntled employee could write about his boss. "The moment I enjoyed most in *Elvis... What Happened?* came when I read that in 1966, Robert Mitchum offered Elvis the lead in *Thunder Road*—a perfect vehicle for Elvis... I enjoyed that moment because I knew that Mitchum had already made *Thunder Road* in 1958, and so could conclude that the rest of the book might be suspect."

*　　*　　*

Out of the distorted memoirs may have come some truth about the reasons behind the sudden departure of Linda Thompson. The story is told that Elvis and his chums were in the Vegas *Hilton*. They were all assembled, sitting in total silence. Elvis sat staring out the window saying nothing. Scattered around him were various books on the occult and religion.

Linda looked at Elvis, then at the men. Her thoughts, for a religious young lady, were probably unprintable. Elvis was a very sick man and it didn't require a one-time lover to recognize it. She took the obvious and only logical action. She called Elvis' doctor who arrived shortly thereafter.

The next morning was probably one of the several times that Elvis was whisked back to Memphis in his private plane and into the Baptist Memorial Hospital.

A hospital attendant said, "He was hospitalized

there from April first to sixth of this year, after cutting short a tour. Elvis was here for two weeks in January and February of 1975, for two weeks in September the same year and for two weeks in 1973.

"They were treating him for everything— hypertension, enlarged colon, gastroenteritis, stomach inflammation. He was getting cortisone treatments. I thought that was for arthritis. One doctor said Elvis might have lupus erythematosus. Lupus is an extremely rare, chronic inflammation of the nervous system, kidneys and skin. It is treated with cortisone. He also had a severe liver condition. Cortisone might have explained his weight—he was a big man—he was weighing at least two hundred and thirty pounds."

This seems to bear out an article in *Elvis: Memories Forever* the magazine from Lorelei Publishing Company which reached the stands first after Elvis' death with his life story and a detailed account of the circumstances of his final hours. The story titled: *The Truth About Drugs, The Guns and The Violence* bore out what everyone believed about Elvis. No one, even of his prominence, could have kept his fans so totally in the dark if he were a dangerous drug user, as implied in *What Happened?*

The piece is reprinted here in full:

"Everybody's been told that Elvis Presley neither drank nor smoked. But according to three of his ex-bodyguards, Delbert and Red West and Dave Hebler, Elvis Presley did take drugs—'to perform, to sleep, to get up—even to go to the bathroom.'

"According to those same sources, he was also an

avid gun collector who 'once bought 32 pistols in one month,' and was so violent he ordered them to kill or find a hit man to get rid of Mike Stone, the man he felt stole wife Priscilla from him. Well, the truth is that Elvis did sometimes take drugs—but were they habit-forming or illegal? As you can see from his most recent picture, Elvis had blown up like a balloon in recent months, and was taking appetite depressants—often known to contain 'speed'—and you can get them legally with a doctor's prescription.

"He was also taking drugs for hypertension, and a twisted colon (the reason he probably needed drugs 'to go to the bathroom'), and the man had hardening of the arteries far beyond what his age would make you imagine. If he were 'over-medicated,' it was a doctor's decision. And if he were also on the usual 'uppers and downers' most performers turn to—sometimes with, sometimes without a doctor's consent—he seems to have definitely not been into hard drugs of any kind. No heroin—nothing addictive.

"As to the stories about his gun mania—all collectors are maniacs of a kind. The question is: Did he ever really use those guns to hurt anyone? The answer is no. But the charge of violence is most serious—especially the threat to Mike Stone's life. That happened, says Red West, back in 1973, when Elvis was so hurt over his wife leaving him. But says Red, it wasn't just an idle threat. Elvis kept after Red until the latter did call a hit man. But once Red told Elvis that he had a deal if he wanted it—Elvis immediately backed down.

"The violence, the wish for revenge, was mostly fantasy, as it would be with most normal folk who'd been hurt. So what is the truth about the drugs, the guns, the violence? The truth is that Elvis was a physically ill man with problems, an avid collector of guns whatever that might mean psychologically— and when he was hurt and unhappy, he had wicked daydreams of revenge like all of us. He never used his power to make that fantasy of revenge come true."

Chapter 13

At the time of his death Elvis was looking forward to a concert tour that was supposed to begin in Portland, Maine. It wasn't odd for the singer to still be in Graceland. He rarely arrived for a concert until just before he was to appear on stage. This time was no different. But he was getting ready for so much more.

You weren't going to find Elvis Presley's name listed in *Variety* as "available." There wasn't a corner of the globe that wouldn't pay the Colonel's fee to have the honor of welcoming Elvis Presley. He was far from a washed-up *has-been* sulking in his palace because "they don't want my style of entertaining any more."

Elvis had changed with the times, and, as the times changed, he would have proved durable. Why? Because it was there. That intangible something known as nothing at all but described as showmanship. And Elvis' big plus—the quality of his voice.

Any doubts about the strength of his vocal chords were dispelled by the posthumous showing of *Elvis In Concert* which was videotaped at concerts in

Nebraska and South Dakota only weeks before he died. A jowled, heavy-set Elvis may have come as a shock to viewers who'd seen only Elvis' old movies and had not attended his concerts in recent years.

But the visual disappointment was quickly dissipated as Elvis moved into his repertory with a voice rich in timbre, absolutely on pitch and not a trace of a wobble. Any professional would tell you that a man of forty-two, singing as well as Presley did a couple of months before he died, had done very little to harm the instrument. Indiscriminate use of drugs or alcohol would have shown.

But there was no avoiding the truth. Elvis was in poor health. The bloat was distracting; the added weight diminished Elvis' footwork, as well as the body movements that had always been his trademark. After forty, Elvis would have been a fool to have attempted recreating the style of *Elvis the Pelvis*. The vaunted grace was missing.

Elvis had reached a point in his career where he would have served his style better in a concert hall than an arena with all the old trappings—the very hugeness of the building, the kaleidoscope of lights, the hawkers selling photos of Elvis, albums with his life story, the hit records, Elvis Presley buttons and pennants. The "side show" money the Colonel had as much respect for as the boxoffice scale. There were times when you felt the atmosphere overwhelming the star.

But there was the other side of the coin. It was hokey—all that and more. But this was an Elvis Presley show and the razzle-dazzle atmosphere of a

Country Fair, the Carnival Midway was what the fans had come to see. They ranged in age from six to sixty plus.

Youngsters wanted to discover what their elders had been talking about all these years. Old fans, grey-haired, coiffed and gussied up for a night with a good friend, expected things to be as they had been before. Back in the fifties when they, like Elvis and the rest of the world, were younger. They hadn't come for the stuffy refinements of an older singer putting on a concert. They wanted a "show"—and Elvis gave it to them, tossing scarves at the audience, reaching down, shaking their hands. They'd come to the performance to love—and to be loved.

The audience reacted from habit, cheering the legend, the illusion. They were grateful to have him there—under any conditions. Who could have imagined that he was a dying man?

In 1975, Barbra Streisand went to Las Vegas to see Elvis perform. Backstage they had a long talk. She told Elvis she was planning a new version of *A Star is Born,* the sturdy perennial that had served both Judy Garland and Janet Gaynor as a memorable vehicle. Barbra's version was to modernize the story, making the lovers a worn-out, has-been Rock Star who helps a young girl on her way up. This would be Streisand.

It was a tempting challenge and, despite the usual reports that the Colonel had stepped in and spiked it with his money demands, Tom Parker was no fool. He knew the picture and the role would have accomplished Presley's ambitions—establishing him as a major, serious dramatic star.

Elvis, supposedly, underwent slight facial surgery to touch up the jowls and bags under his eyes, but his health was such that Colonel Parker, probably, had the wisdom to know Elvis would break under the strain of a huge motion picture assignment, particularly under the conditions that went with Barbra Streisand.

Not that the Colonel doubted for a moment that he'd be able to handle Barbra Streisand. She was supposed to know the whole "bit"—but her experience was strictly Broadway and Hollywood. She'd never bumped into a southern carnival man.

As a theatrical venture and publicity side show it was full of promise and once-in-a-generation chemistry. That it didn't come off was hardly a professional tragedy for Elvis. It might have been a new and exciting mountain. But hadn't he climbed so many peaks already?

He's left an extraordinary legacy of movies, records, television and concert appearances— certainly more than any entertainer of his age. But they went far beyond quantity. They pleased people. They entertained. The critics hissed and snarled. Who gave a damn? Elvis, perhaps. The Colonel, never. The public seldom bothered to read the reviews anyhow. They'd been around the route before—in the early days when Elvis made the front pages with his sexy, swinging hips, the leer, the boyish smile, the sultry sexiness he exuded.

*   *   *

Elvis deserved a better personal life than he found. Not that for a time it wasn't great fun, being the king, the Sultan, the kid who had everything. On the outside he gave the illusion of a man perfectly content with his way of life, his image, fame, money. Why not? Once he'd been the country kid with nothing, one pair of shoes with holes in the soles, who grabbed the brass ring of success and never let it out of his grasp.

Show business success, when it comes fast and big, has been compared at times with a skyrocket. But skyrockets fall to earth once they burn out. Elvis Presley never burned out. He was like the tightwire performer equipped with skill, balance and judgment that is granted to very few. Luck alone will not suffice. Moreover, there was always Colonel Parker there to make sure that his "boy" always got the best.

In many respects he did. In others, Colonel Parker's love affair with money sold his "boy" out too cheaply. This certainly was true toward the end of Elvis' flick career when no one gave a damn what was put on celluloid, as long as Presley was paid a salary of a million dollars a picture, a percentage of the profits, and his companies owned the sound tracks.

This was ruthless exploitation of a talent in a medium that required more than Elvis could bring to it on the spot. It took more than learning lines to be a movie star; it required the art of projecting emotions, feeling things, digging reality—not the glitter of the platform, the lights, the gaudy hurly-burly world of Colonel Parker's Midway where Elvis was the *Wonder Boy of the Century*—the *Greatest Entertainer on the Face of the Earth.*

* * *

Standing way up there on his pedestal, it was lonely. Elvis said so. He had become the prisoner of his fame—unable to walk the streets without being mobbed. He couldn't go to restaurants, shopping or even to the movies. Only once when he was making the Christmas *special* did one of the producers persuade the star to take a walk along Sunset Strip. It was a surprise—no one noticed him.

Ah, but the producer noticed that Elvis raised his voice. He talked more loudly. What was wrong? No attention? No mob? Had the King abdicated? It annoyed him. He was so used to adulation that it had become a necessity. Part of the Presley presence.

How much then of his vaunted loneliness was real? How much imagined? How much really reflected Elvis' inner wishes? We will never know. He seemed to be candid, but there was always that air of mystery about him. Interviews were granted only when Colonel Parker felt disposed. No matter how glibly he talked, Elvis appeared to be holding back.

Sometimes they were strictly professional. Often he talked about his belief, the religious faith he'd learned from his mother. This was real. He'd never lost sight of those values. Or he'd be as frank as he could about his marital break-up.

What angered—and hurt—Elvis the most was that Priscilla had left him for another man. It wasn't bad enough that career ambitions had separated them, hers as well as his. But another man! That was unthinkable in Presley's world. You just didn't walk out on the King! This represented the tragic flaw in Elvis' "royal" character, the point where he believed his own publicity.

When they married, was there really more than the faintest glimmer of hope that it would stand as the "eternal flame of love" they declared they were seeking? Not likely. After so many years, there wasn't much Elvis and Priscilla didn't know about the other. Priscilla wanted to be a modern woman, not a Memphis housewife. She had no intention of being tied down, yet Elvis was the guy who had said he'd found a girl who was "just like Mom." Here and there you find hints this was what he wanted to believe. Then, he was living in a world of illusion, crediting Priscilla with qualities that never existed in the first place. He wanted to believe they were there, and when he woke up to the truth, it was the shock of his life.

Life had failed him when it deprived him of his mother. Life failed him a second time when he lost the one woman he presumed would become her substitute.

Presley writers are reduced to stuttering when it comes to listing the lovely ladies of the screen who drifted in and out of Elvis' life—as casually as a summer's breeze. The ground rules were always the same. Elvis was never unchivalrous. He remained a southern gentleman. Still it became harder and harder to swallow the stories issuing with monotonous regularity from Hollywood that the most devastating dolls on the face of the earth couldn't hold Elvis in their nets for longer than a few weeks.

Elvis turned wolf-man later than most—the surest sign of loneliness. He started grabbing pleasure on the run, finding it in short takes rather than giving himself totally to one girl who would truly love him. It was the mark of the desperate man. When the man is a public idol, his name a household word, his face known all over the world, how much more difficult it must have been?

Sometimes the thought occurs that perhaps Elvis felt safest being caged behind the walls of Graceland, that the bodyguards who surrounded him as he made his way to the stage were guardians of this curious predisposition to always enjoy protection.

*   *   *

I very much doubt that theatrical historians are going to take seriously the *penny-dreadful* exposé of Elvis' private life by a *furriner* like Steve Dunleavy whose knowledge of America was so limited that he couldn't differentiate between poor and "poor white trash." Perhaps someone in the future will explore Elvis' intimate life and come up with even murkier secrets than Dunleavy's petty peek.

Does it make a difference?

Not likely.

Elvis came out of the south carrying his unique brand of rock 'n' roll with traces of white "rockability" and black "rhythm blues"—the music he'd learned at camp meetings, revivals and church conventions and from the thumping of pianos he heard hanging around Memphis' Beale Street.

He dressed it up in a duck tail and sideburns, in glittering sequins, in bright colors, strummed a guitar, swung his hips and woke up a whole generation, carrying them with him out of the inertia of the fifties.

He got there first and lasted longest—the blatantly sexual entertainer who heard and suffered jeers and humiliation when he travelled north of the Mason-Dixon line, but who had the guts to hold on. With time and young people on his side, he turned their shock into love and admiration.

He gave men's clothes an easy informality for which grandfathers were grateful. He spurred the sales of guitars and got street kids interested in music—a feat the social agencies overlooked when they branded him as a menace to young womanhood.

Elvis broke every existing record in the theatrical books. His records were blockbusters, so were his concerts and his TV *specials*. Even the tawdry collection of films he appeared in earned millions for his producers—new fans for Elvis. A fortune and a King-like life style for Elvis.

Elvis' handsome looks became the model for young males just as they'd beguiled their girl friends who discovered him first. Part choirboy and part outlaw, he brought a "new look" to the American male which it could certainly afford after years of the Coolidge and Hoover high collar, the Roosevelt cape, Truman's corset and the broad-brimmed hats of L.B.J. Not to mention the grey flannel suit.

He made it possible for the President of the United States to wander around his peanut farm in blue jeans and wear a sweater in the White House while giving a *Fireside Chat*. President Carter understood Elvis and his world; inevitably he joined his countrymen in sympathizing with the family's loss.

Elvis also brought healthy sexuality to music which had lived too long in the world of "tea for two," "moons that turned blue" and "four leaf clovers" that horticulturists had learned to grow anyhow.

Elvis was the King because he embodied all the good points of sex as well as the bad ones. He could make it appear grand or vulgar—with the swing of his hips, the leer on his lips. He was never lonely strumming and entertaining the screaming fans.

They were the source of his strength, they felt most of his love. No wonder his life was brutally lonely. When he started out he was all on his own. Way back in his school days when his odd clothes, long hair and sideburns made him "different," there was no one to champion, no one to chart a course or guide him. Elvis was alone—the mud of the Mississippi on his shoes, the beat of a new generation in his heart. It took time, energy, patience and guts to say what he wanted to the world.

Little Lisa Marie can grow up knowing her father gave back to us everything that we gave him. The white Cadillacs were only symbols of our love. He sang for us. He challenged us to change. He never cheated. He always gave his best. We loved him very much.

Elvis Presley was a decent man.

About the Author

David Hanna was born in Philadelphia and began his international career as a journalist in Hollywood, covering the Golden Age of the movies, the 40's and 50's for the *Hollywood Reporter* and the *Los Angeles Daily News*. He began travelling in 1952 and for 20 years covered the International Scene, Jet-Set Society, politics and the underworld for the *London Daily Express, New York Times, Herald-Tribune, Coronet Magazine, Cosmopolitan, King Features* and many others. His articles have been translated into a dozen languages. He edited *Confidential, Whisper* and *Uncensored* and now lives in New York City.

In the past four years, Hanna has written more than two dozen paperback books, covering Hollywood personalities, the underworld, and publications. His film biographies have included works on Mae West, Robert Redford, and profiles of John Wayne, James Stewart, Henry Fonda and Gary Cooper.

He is also the author of *Second Chance,* a study of alcoholism and the famous personalities who have come out of the "closet" to help others with the same problem.